ETERNAL FRANCE

ETERNAL FRANCE

216 PICTURES IN PHOTOGRAVURE
BY MARTIN HÜRLIMANN

WITH
AN APPRECIATION BY
PAUL VALÉRY

AND
HISTORICAL NOTES

LONDON · THAMES AND HUDSON · NEW YORK

First Published 1952
Second Impression 1953

PRODUCED BY THAMES AND HUDSON LTD LONDON AND ATLANTIS VERLAG ZURICH
PRINTED IN GREAT BRITAIN BY JARROLD AND SONS LTD NORWICH
GRAVURE PLATES PRINTED BY ETS BRAUN ET CIE MULHOUSE

AN APPRECIATION OF FRANCE

BY PAUL VALÉRY

THERE is no nation more frank; there is certainly none more mysterious than the French. There is no nation so easy for the stranger to observe, or that more readily leads him to suppose that he has got to know her at the first encounter. Later he will realize that there is none whose movements are more difficult to foresee, or whose reactions may be more surprising. In history we see her constantly playing an extreme rôle; she alternates between the heights and the abysses with greater frequency and in greater amplitude than any other country. Indeed the fitful light of the many storms through which she has passed leaves in the mind a picture which on reflection we perceive to be a fairly accurate representation of the reality; we come to feel that the function of this country, both through its inherent qualities and through its structure, has been to act physically and historically as a kind of gyroscope, maintaining a curious stability, though subject more than once a century to secular oscillations, resulting from the vicissitudes inseparable from life itself, from explosions within the body, and from the storms and political tremors that assail it from without.

France arises, she stumbles and falls, picks herself up and goes carefully, recovers her greatness; France tears herself to pieces and regains her energies; she is in turn proud, resigned, indifferent and enthusiastic, whilst always standing out amongst the nations for her curiously personal character. Highly strung and full of contrasting elements, the French nation has discovered in these contrasts wholly unforeseen sources of strength; possibly the secret of her prodigious powers of resistance resides in the great range of her varying qualities. With the levity of character which the French display they combine singular flexibility and powers of endurance. A charming ease of intercourse is closely associated in their case with a powerful critical faculty which is always on the alert. France is perhaps the only country where ridicule has proved to be a factor in history. In France ridicule has undermined and overthrown Governments; an epigram or a happy, sometimes too happy, turn of phrase, has in a few moments ruined, in the public esteem, powers that were strongly entrenched. The French moreover display a certain unruliness which, however, yields at once to discipline where it is apparent that discipline is required. On occasion the nation will suddenly achieve unity just when one might have expected to find her divided.

*

It is clear that it is particularly difficult to arrive at a simple definition of the French nation, and this difficulty is in itself a not unimportant constituent of the definition. In describing it we are bound to attribute characteristics which clash with each other. I shall attempt directly to make clear the reasons for this. But in discussing France, or any other political entity of the same order, it is never an easy thing to visualize exactly what one means by a *nation*. The most obvious and commonest characteristics of a nation escape the notice of the people of the country, who are unaware of that which has always been before their eyes. To the stranger who sees them they loom disproportionately large, and he is not conscious of that multitude of intimate characteristics and invisible realities which go to accomplish the mystery of the deep union of millions of men.

There are therefore two main paths to self-deception on the subject of any particular nation.

Moreover the general idea itself of a *nation* is not easy to grasp. The mind is bewildered by the widely diverse aspects of this idea; it hesitates between very different ways of expressing it. No sooner has a satisfying formula apparently been found, than it suggests some particular case which it does not cover.

The idea of a nation is as familiar in use, and as real to the mind, as it is complex and elusive on reflection. But is this not so with many words of primary importance? The words *law, race, property*, etc., fall easily from our lips. What is law? What is race? What is property? *We know and we do not know!*

Thus all these potent ideas, which are both abstract and vital, and which at times exert an intense and dominating influence over us, all these terms which in the minds of peoples and statesmen go to make up the thoughts, the schemes, the projects, and the decisions on which depend the destiny, the prosperity, the ruin, the life or death of human beings are in the light of reflection vague and imperfect symbols. And yet when men make use of these indefinable ideas among themselves, they understand each other perfectly. Thus they attain superficial clarity for the purpose of communication between men; although they are obscure and infinitely differentiated to the individual mind. This paradoxical conclusion has led me rather away from my subject, but it has perhaps been worth the little loss of time which has been involved in calling attention to this fact.

There still remain one or two generalities for me to touch upon before speaking especially of France.

Between a country and the people who inhabit it, between man and his surroundings, the surface, the contour, the rivers, the climate, the fauna and flora, the substance of the earth, there gradually form reciprocal relationships, which increase in number and complexity, in proportion to the length of time during which the people have been in the country.

If the nation be a composite one, formed of successive influxes through the ages, the combinations of relationships multiply.

To the observer, these mutual reactions between the land which is mother or nurse, and the organized life which she supports and nourishes, are not all equally apparent. For some consist of the various modifications which human life imposes on a country, and others of the influence which their dwelling-place has upon the inhabitants; and although the influence of mankind upon the earth is always obvious and easy to interpret, the inverse is nearly always impossible to assess in its separate elements or to define exactly. Man exploits the soil—clears it, digs it, sows seed, cuts down trees, builds, makes roads through the mountains, harnesses the waters, introduces new species. It is possible to note the processes by which he has carried out works, brought land under cultivation and changed the face of nature. But the manner in which man is changed by his habitat is as obscure as the fact is certain. The effects upon the living creature of the heavens, the waters, the air that he breathes, the prevailing winds, the food he eats, etc., lie within the realm of physiological and psychological phenomena, whereas the results of his actions are generally on the plane of the physical or mechanical. The greater number of our operations upon nature are recognizable; the artificial is generally an encroachment upon nature, but the pervasive action of nature upon us is action upon herself, and its results become incorporated in our being. Anything that acts upon a creature without subduing it produces a form of life, or a more or less stable variety of life.

These simple observations indicate that knowledge of a country requires two kinds of research of varying difficulty; as in many other matters it is apparent that the more important things for us to understand are also the more difficult. Manners, ideals and politics, products of the mind, are imponderable results produced by an infinitely intricate network of causes, where the mind is lost amongst a number of independent factors and their combinations, towards the elucidation of which even statistics are hopelessly incapable of contributing. *Such supreme impotence is of fatal significance to mankind.* Here, much more than in any conflict of interest, is the cause of that which brings nations into opposition, proving itself an obstacle to any general organization of human beings on the earth, such has been vainly attempted in the past through the spirit either of conquest, religion or revolution, each acting in accordance with its own nature. Man knows too little of man to refrain from having recourse to experiments. Crude, futile or desperate solutions are suggested or imposed upon the human race just as upon individuals—*because they have not knowledge.* Nations are foreign to one another, just as individuals of varying characters, ages, beliefs, customs and requirements are different. They survey one another with uneasy curiosity; they smile and sulk, they admire a detail and imitate it;

constantly being drafted in over a period of centuries; these were followed by swarms of Moors and Saracens. Greeks or Phœnicians, Latins and Saracens coming up from the South as the Northmen came from the Channel coast and the Atlantic, entered the country in numbers that were not very considerable. The great mass of newcomers were probably those brought in on the tides of the East.

However that may be, a map illustrating the movements of peoples in the same way as the dispositions of the atmosphere are shown on a meteorological chart, would reveal the country of France as resembling a region of the air in which the currents of humanity have been set in motion, mingled, diffused and resolved as the resulting eddies have become increasingly interwoven and blended.

Thus the fundamental factor in the formation of France has been the blending of a remarkable number of different racial elements present in her territory. All the nations of Europe are composite, *and there is perhaps none in which only one language is spoken.* But I believe there is none whose racial and linguistic formula is so rich as that of France. She has arrived at her peculiar individuality through the complex phenomenon of internal exchange and of the individual alliances which have been effected within her between so many variations of race and temperament. The combinations resulting from so many independent factors and the admixture of their inherited qualities account for many of the inconsistencies in the acts and feelings of the French, and the remarkable standard mean of the individual Frenchman. *When we consider the highly differentiated strains which go to make up the French nation, and out of which she has constituted in the course of some centuries so complete and clearly defined a European personality producing an individualized culture and spirit, we are reminded of a tree which has been many times engrafted so that its quality and the flavour of its fruit result from the happy combination of highly varying saps and juices uniting into one single and indivisible whole.*

This fact also makes it possible for us to understand most of the specifically French institutions and organizations, these being the resultant of very powerful reactions by the body of the nation in support of its unity. Feeling for this vital unity is excessively strong in France.

Were I to allow myself to be enticed into such reflections as are dignified by the fine name of historical philosophy, I might perhaps indulge in the speculation that all truly great events in French history were either actions which have threatened or tended to disturb a certain equilibrium between races that has been effected within a certain territorial area, or reactions, occasionally of peculiar intensity, corresponding to such assaults and tending to re-establish such equilibrium.

Sometimes the nation seems to be endeavouring to achieve or regain her "optimum" composition that is best adapted to her internal system of compromise, and to annexe her full and complete life; at other times she seems to be endeavouring to regain the unity which her very composition renders essential. In her acute internal struggle it is always the party which seems to be in the way of re-establishing threatened unity at the earliest possible moment and at any cost, that has every chance of victory. That is why the dramatic crises in French history especially are identified with a few great names, names of persons, of families or of assemblies which have with particular emphasis stood for this essential tendency in moments of crisis or of reorganization. Whether we speak of the Capets, Jeanne d'Arc, Louis XI, Henri IV, Richelieu, the Convention or Napoleon—we call to mind the same thing—a symbol of national identity and unity in action.

*

Now, as I think over all these representative names, another comes to my mind, the name of a town. Surely there is nothing more significant, or that more aptly illustrates what I have just said, than the enormous advance during the centuries of the pre-eminence of Paris; surely there is nothing more typical than the powerful attraction which she exerts, and the constant force that emanates from her as from a vital centre whose functions transcend by far those merely of a political capital or of a city of the first magnitude. Paris has with patent consistency definitely tended through a jealous and intense concentration to harmonize the great regional and individual differences of France. The increase during the last two centuries in the number of the institutions through which Paris exerts her influence upon the life of France may certainly be referred to the growing necessity of co-ordinating the whole, and to the recent union with more distant provinces having more varied traditions. At the outbreak of the Revolution France was already centralized in her Government; the Court already gave the lead in matters of taste and conduct. The centralization hardly concerned directly any but the leisured and governing classes. But when the revolutionary assemblies met, and during the critical years which followed, there ensued an active flow of men and ideas between Paris and the rest of France. Local affairs, schemes and denunciations, come to Paris, together with the men who are most active or ambitious, and fermentation is set up. Paris in its turn inundates the country with delegates, decrees and newspapers; with the products of the many meetings, incidents, passions and discussions, which all the different elements that she has attracted to jostle one another within her boundaries have engendered inside her walls.

I do not know why historians as a rule fail to emphasize what I feel to be a great fact, the transformation of Paris into a central organ, capable of facing the world as a compact whole; an organ not merely political and administrative, but also an organ for shaping, maturing and enunciating judgments, a determining influence upon the general mind of the country. Possibly they shrink from classing as an event, a phenomenon of comparatively slow development to which no precise date can be assigned. Yet it is necessary occasionally to endow historical vision with freedom in regard to space and time that we have gained from the use of optical instruments and moving pictures. Imagine that you can see in the space of a few minutes that which has taken centuries to come about; that you see Paris taking shape and growing, ever increasing her contact with the country roundabout and growing rich; Paris becoming essential as a centre which maintains the circulation of the whole, her indispensability and her administrative power growing more and more marked, and increasing with the Revolution, with the Empire, and with the development of railways, or telegraphic communication, of the press, and what we may call *intensive literature* . . . You will then apprehend *Paris as an event,* an event fully comparable to the foundation of an institution of capital importance, and to all the significant events which history registers and deplores.

No event more significant has occurred. I have indicated how it has come about. That great city, to which a whole great nation delegates all its spiritual powers, and through which it elaborates its fundamental conventions in matters of taste and conduct—a typical product of France and of France's extraordinary diversity—serves as an intermediary or interpreter to represent her in her relations to the rest of the world; while enabling the rest of the world to form a rapid, inaccurate and delightful acquaintance with France as a whole.

*

The ideas about France which I have developed above, or rather suggested to the reader, as a mere approximation to reality, arose in my mind as a remote consequence of some remarks which I made a very long time ago on a perfectly definite matter.

I have sometimes concerned myself with poetry; not only have I spent some years of my life in composing poems; I have quite frequently indulged in an examination of the nature and methods of the poetic art generally.

Now, when one comes to consider the physical attributes of poetry, as in its relation to music, proceeding to a comparison of the metres and verse forms of various peoples, one cannot fail to perceive a fact which has tended to escape comment and discussion just because it is pretty generally known and very obvious.

Musically, French poetry differs from all other poetry, so much so that it has sometimes been considered almost entirely deficient in many of those means to beauty which are available to the poet in other languages. I am of the opinion that this is a mistaken belief; but as is so often the case, this belief is an illegitimate and subjective deduction from a perfectly correct observation. We should turn to a consideration of the language itself and see wherein its phonetic peculiarity consists; when this has been determined we can endeavour to find the reason for it.

There are three characteristics that clearly distinguish French from other Western languages. In *well-spoken* French there is practically *no variation of pitch*; its sentences fall within a narrower register, and its individual words are flatter than in other languages. French consonants are remarkably soft, there being no harsh or guttural sounds. There is no French consonant that any European cannot pronounce correctly. French vowel sounds are numerous, having very fine shades of difference; they constitute a rare and valuable assemblage of subtle variations furnishing those poets who are worthy of the name with *sound values*, through the interplay of which they can make up for the slightness of the register and the general moderation of stress in their language; the varieties of *è* and *é*, the rich diphthongs such as *feuille*, *rouille*, *faille*, *pleure*, *toise*, *tien*, etc., and the mute *e* which may have a real existence, or may be barely perceptible and practically faded out altogether, so that the most subtle variations of pure silence is the result, while enduing the end of many words with a kind of penumbra, the projection as it were of an accented syllable. A vast number of examples could be cited to demonstrate how effectively these characteristics can be used.

I have, however, mentioned them only in order to support the contention which I have just put forward, that the French language is in a class apart, being phonetically as distinct from the so-called Latin or Romance as it is from the Germanic languages.

It is particularly remarkable that the language of a country lying between Italy and Spain should move within a register much narrower than that of the Italian or Spanish languages. Its vowel sounds are more numerous, and have finer shades of difference, while its consonants are never so strong, and never require so much physical effort to pronounce as in other Latin languages.

A consideration of the history of French reveals certain facts, which seem to be significant in this connection. We find for instance that although the letter *r*, being neither rolled nor aspirated, is not at all harsh in French, it has frequently threatened to disappear from the language and to be replaced through a continued softening process by some milder sound. Thus, the word *chaire* has become *chaise*, etc.

In short, even a superficial phonetic study, such as is practicable for a mere *amateur*, has revealed to me characteristics and peculiarities in the French language, and in French poetry, which I can only explain as being a consequence of those very national characteristics to which I have just referred.

The fact that French is moderate in its use of stress and pitch; that to speak without an "accent" is to speak French well; that over-harsh or emphatic elements are barred, or have been gradually eliminated; that its sound variations are complex, and its muted letters have such a perceptible quality, can I think be explained only by the manner in which the language has been formed into a highly complex amalgam. In a country where Celts, Latins and German peoples have achieved a very intimate fusion, and in which a number of different idioms are current as well as the dominant language—various Latin languages, and the French, Breton, Basque and Catalonian dialects—a linguistic unity has proved to be essential as a counterpart to political and spiritual unity. Such unity could only be achieved by systematic compromise and mutual concession inducing modifications by dispensing with what others could not pronounce. It is perhaps possible to carry this argument further, and to consider whether the specific forms of French may not be attributable to the same requirements.

The clarity of structure of the language of France—were it possible to define it by so simple a name—would appear to result from the same needs and the same conditions; neither can it be doubted that the literature of the country in its most characteristic features similarly results from an agglomeration of very different qualities, being of highly diverse origins forced into a scheme which has to be all the more clearly defined as its component parts are various. Pascal and Voltaire, Lamartine and Hugo, Musset and Mallarmé are products of the same country. A few years ago you might have met Emile Zola and Théodore de Bainville, in the same salon, or if you wished to visit two extremes you could have gone in a quarter of an hour from Anatole France's study to J. K. Huysman's office.

This is the natural place to consider what characteristically French contribution France has made to Letters. We should for instance bring out the remarkable development of the critical faculty as applied to matters *of form*, which has been an important feature since the sixteenth century; literature was dominated during the period by the spirit which we call classical, and it has never since ceased to exercise a direct or an indirect influence upon literary work.

France is possibly the only country where considerations of pure form and a regard for *form in itself* have persisted as dominating factors in modern times. A passionate feeling for form seems to be most frequently developed in conjunction with a keen critical sense and a sceptical attitude of mind. Indeed we find it associated with particular freedom in the treatment of the subject matter, and a kind of sense of irony in general. These qualities or vices are usually cultivated in social surroundings that offer a large variety of contrasting experiences, so that the exchange of conflicting ideas is concentrated and intensified until it acquires the brilliance and sometimes the extreme dryness of a flame. The parts played in French literature by the Court and by Paris were and are of primary importance. France's outstanding literary achievement is perhaps her abstract prose, which has no counterpart elsewhere. But I cannot expound these views fully here; I should require a whole book for the purpose.

I would add but one further observation to this wholly inadequate sketch; foundations such as the French Academy, and institutions such as the Comédie Française, are each in its own particular way specifically national products, the essential function of which is to confirm and sanctify, and indeed to give an expression apparent to France herself, of her powerful and voluntary *unity*.

*

Before leaving the reader to enjoy the varied collection of pictures in this book, and before liberating him from these abstract or exploratory ideas, letting him devote himself to the simple pleasure of using his eyes, I must say something about our art. I shall confine myself to a few words on French architecture, with the aim of demonstrating its originality during the great epochs when it flourished. If we are to understand French architecture from 1100 to 1800 A.D. —seven centuries, each one of which has contributed its masterpieces and its several categories of masterpieces: cathedrals, châteaux, palaces, a remarkable series—we can only do so in the light of the most elusive and the most fundamental principle of art, that the intimate harmony between the medium and the design should find the fullest expression possible in the nature of the case.

The indissoluble combination of these two elements is incontestably the aim of all great art. Poetry furnishes the simplest illustration of this truth, the intimate union or mysterious symbiosis of sound and meaning being essential to it.

To the extent to which it can achieve such an intimate relationship, which comes into being and completes itself within the depths of the artist's own personality, and in a sense takes possession of *his whole body*, the work of art acquires some resemblance to the living products of nature in which the life forces cannot be disassociated from the forms in which they are expressed.

In the case of architecture, in order truly to appreciate it, and that it may yield us a higher degree of pleasure, we must learn to distinguish those constructions in which design and substance have remained independent of one another from those in which these two elements have become more or less inseparably combined. The public too often confuses genuinely architectural qualities with decorative effects that are purely external. People are content to be moved, astonished or amused by theatrical effects, and there are undoubtedly some very beautiful works which delight the eye, although they are made of coarse material such as plaster imitations, applied marbles on inferior foundations, and trivial ornamentation. *Such erections have no life.* They are masks and counterfeits concealing the sorry reality. On the other hand an understanding critic has but to survey a simple village church, of which thousands can still be found in France, to be stirred suddenly in his fundamental emotions and to perceive to a certain degree the *feeling of synthesis*.

Our architects of the great periods have always *visually* conceived their buildings at one stroke, and not in two separate spiritual *moments* or in two series of operations, one having reference to the medium, and the other to the design. If I may use the expression, they used to think in materials. Moreover the magnificent quality of the stone in districts where mediaeval architecture developed in its greatest purity, made it easy to conceive the work in this way. If we survey the course of discoveries and achievements effected in this connection between the twelfth and fourteenth centuries, we shall be introduced to a highly remarkable evolutionary process which may be interpreted as a conflict between an increasingly ambitious imagination and design combined with a growing desire for lightness, phantasy and richness on the one hand, and on the other, a feeling for the medium and its qualities, which is not departed from until the end of this great period. This development is marked by an increase in the science of cutting and shaping stone, culminating in some astonishing achievements, and in the abuses inseparable from an excessive virtuosity.

But before this decadence set in, what a number of masterpieces, and what wonderful balance between the various factors making up a building had been achieved! Art has never approximated so closely to the logical grace of living creatures—I mean of such creatures as are successful products of nature—as in those fine works which, differing profoundly from those whose artistic value is comparable merely to that of stage scenery, arouse and even compel one to reflection and a sense of movement. It is a curious fact that we know absolutely nothing of the methods, the technical and theoretic culture, or the mathematical knowledge of their great creators.

I would point out incidentally two very important characteristics in their work which throw a clear light upon what I have just said regarding their manner of conceiving it. Enter Notre-Dame at Paris and survey the section of the building contained between any two pillars of the nave. This section constitutes a whole. It may be compared with a segment of the vertebrae. Structurally and decoratively it is a complete integral element and *visibly* complete. If on the other hand you apply your mind to the outlines, the details of the aisles, of the mouldings, the nerves, the string-courses and the quoins which carry your eye with them in their movement, the impression resulting from an understanding of these ancillary elements, in themselves so simple, may be compared to that conveyed through music by the art of modulation and of imperceptibly carrying the hearer from one mood of the spirit to another. But these higher qualities are not necessarily peculiar to large buildings. A chapel, or a very simply built house, is enough to evoke them, and provides in thousands of villages an enduring witness illustrating the intimate harmony between form and medium through which even quite a lowly structure acquires the character of a spontaneous product of the ground on which it is built.

*

In view of all that I have said, the reader will not be surprised to learn that I regard France herself as a *form*, and that she seems to me to be a *work*. We may say of the French nation that it is man-made, and that it has in a way been designed and constructed like a face whose various parts form themselves into an individual. We may say of France that she is a kind of *law* conferred upon a particular territory and a particular ethnological combination of races, upon a collection of human beings which will consistently organize and reorganize itself throughout the ages in accordance with that law. The most obvious result of the law regulating the existence of France is, as I have said above, the function of Paris and the peculiarity of the part played by her. This phenomenal capital was absolutely necessary in a country which is not marked out by a dominant race, nor by traditions or beliefs, nor by economic circumstances, but by an equilibrium of highly complex factors, an extraordinarily rich diversity and an association of varying climates and inhabitants, requiring as a counterpart a highly powerful co-ordinating instrument.

The characteristics of the French nation are pretty well known. The French are quick-witted, generally prudent in their actions, variable on the surface, but constant and faithful in their deeper feelings. They may easily be heedless of tradition, but are deeply rooted in their habits; they are both sagacious and trivial, discerning and careless, exceedingly restrained, moderate in their real wants, indeed almost excessively so in a period in which overweening ambition and monstrously inflated appetites generally prevail. The Frenchman is content with little. He has no great material wants, and his instincts are temperate. Indeed he regards mechanical development and progress on such lines with a certain scepticism, so that while he often comes to create something, he may then fall asleep over his work, leaving to others the trouble and the profit of exploiting it. Perhaps the French instinctively feel the loss in general spiritual values that may result from the unlimited growth of organization and specialization.

This last characteristic is a natural corollary of the general thesis put forward in this short essay. Without profoundly changing in character it would obviously be impossible for an essentially heterogeneous people, the unification of whose internal differences is a condition of its life, to acquire the uniform and absolutely disciplined way of living suited to nations whose industrial system and "standardized" wants are conditions or ideals corresponding to their nature.

Contrast, even of the most pronounced kind, is almost essential to France. Though religious indifference is so general, she is also the country of the most recent miracles. During the very years in which Renan was developing his method of criticism, and positivism and agnosticism were on the increase, a vision appeared in the Grotto of Lourdes. A Basilica was built there. It is possible that in the country of Voltaire and such as he, the Faith is most seriously and firmly held, and the Orders are recruiting most speedily, while the Church has conferred the largest number of canonizations in France in recent years. But there is little superstition; I mean less than elsewhere. We hear less of telepathy, of psychical research, of materializations and magical cures in France than in some countries which are not so superficial; though I do not say that we hear nothing of these things.

PUBLISHER'S NOTE

A NUMBER of years have passed since Dr. Martin Hürlimann brought his first collection of photographs of France to the notice of Paul Valéry. After leafing through the albums with mounting interest the eminent French man of letters readily agreed to write an introduction to the book which Dr. Hürlimann was then planning. Valéry's literary output is relatively small, but everything he wrote bears the hallmark of a crystal-clear intelligence and a deeply intuitive mind. The appreciation of his own country which he proceeded to write is no exception, and it is still so valid and so pertinent today that we have no hesitation in letting it serve as introduction to this entirely new volume.

Dr. Hürlimann, who travelled the length and breadth of France, both prior to and since the second World War, in his search for the most representative and most telling material for this pictorial anthology, writes in his capacity as photographer and editor of the Swiss edition: "France is a glorious land in which to travel, above all for the curious who, turning aside from the popular tourist routes with their cosmopolitan caravanserais, are anxious to discover 'unknown France'. There, too, he is most likely to win access to the people; for, in order truly to experience these landscapes and buildings, it is necessary to share with her inhabitants the bread and wine which are among the most delicious gifts of 'doulce France'. It is my sincere hope that many who take up this book will be encouraged to follow, each in his own fashion, the paths to which it points the way. . . .

"In the picture sequence we start out from Paris and trace a wide loop across Burgundy, following in turn the Alps and the Mediterranean coast, as far as the Pyrenees; then pass north-eastwards through the central mountain area and along the Atlantic coast as far as the Loire, into Britanny and Normandy, and finally through northern France into the frontier districts of Alsace and Lorraine."

ETERNAL FRANCE

UNE ROUTE NATIONALE

PARIS. LA TOUR EIFFEL

PARIS. NOTRE-DAME

PARIS. PLACE DE LA CONCORDE  4

PARIS. LOUVRE 5

PARIS. LE DOME DES INVALIDES

PARIS. ILE ST-LOUIS

PARIS. PONT ROYAL

8

PARIS. CITÉ UNIVERSITAIRE

PARIS. MUSÉE D'ART MODERNE

10

EGLISE DU RAINCY

11

PARIS. ST-GERMAIN-DES-PRÉS

CHATEAU DE CHANTILLY

CHANTILLY, LE PARC DU CHATEAU

CHATEAU DE VERSAILLES. SALON DE LA GUERRE

CHATEAU DE VERSAILLES

PARC DU CHATEAU DE VERSAILLES

VERSAILLES. LE GRAND TRIANON

18

RAMBOUILLET

19

PALAIS DE FONTAINEBLEAU

20

PALAIS DE FONTAINEBLEAU. SALLE DU CONSEIL

21

PALAIS DE COMPIÈGNE. BIBLIOTHÈQUE DE NAPOLÉON Ier

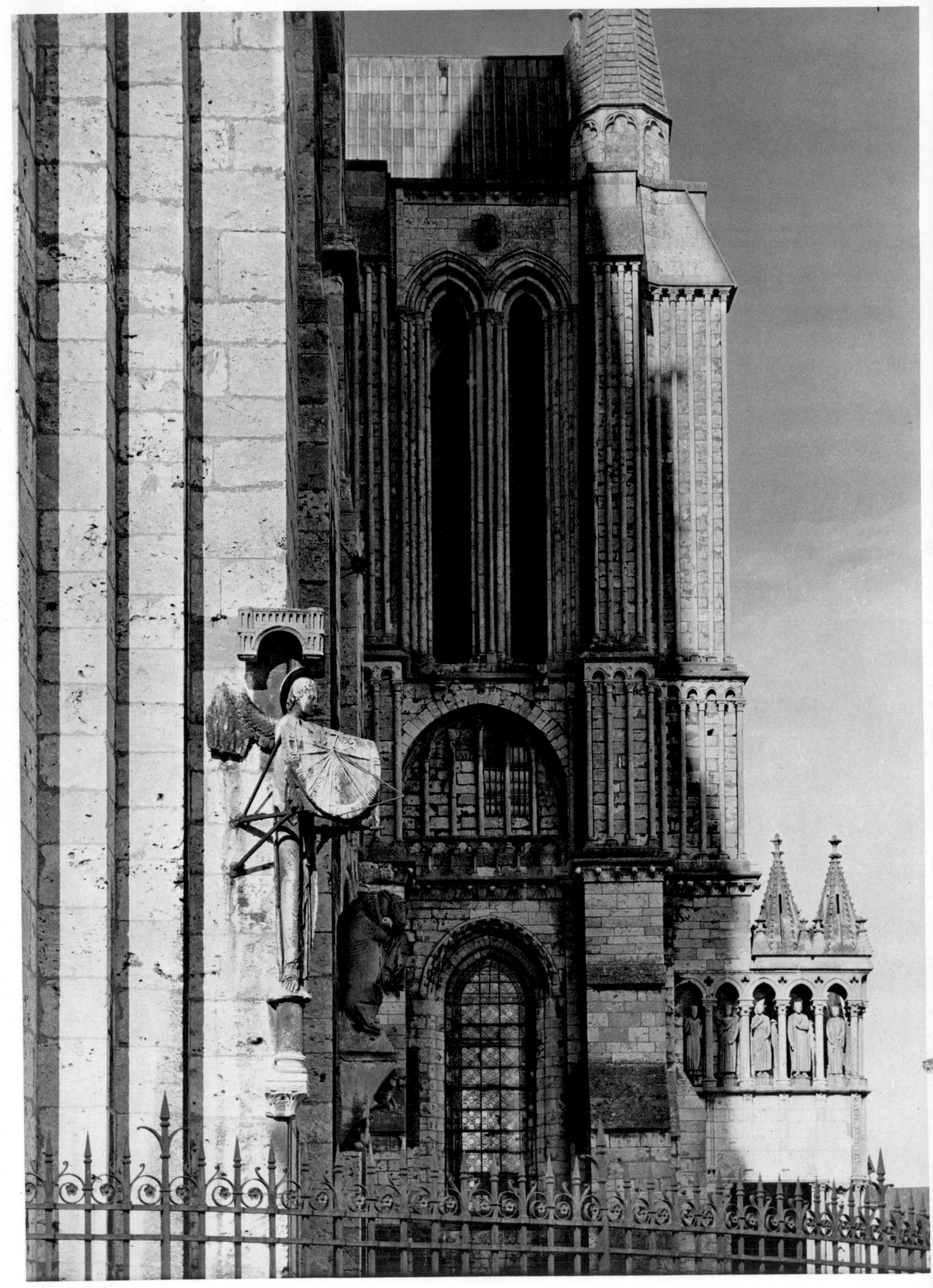

CATHÉDRALE DE CHARTRES

CHARTRES

24

EN BEAUCE

25

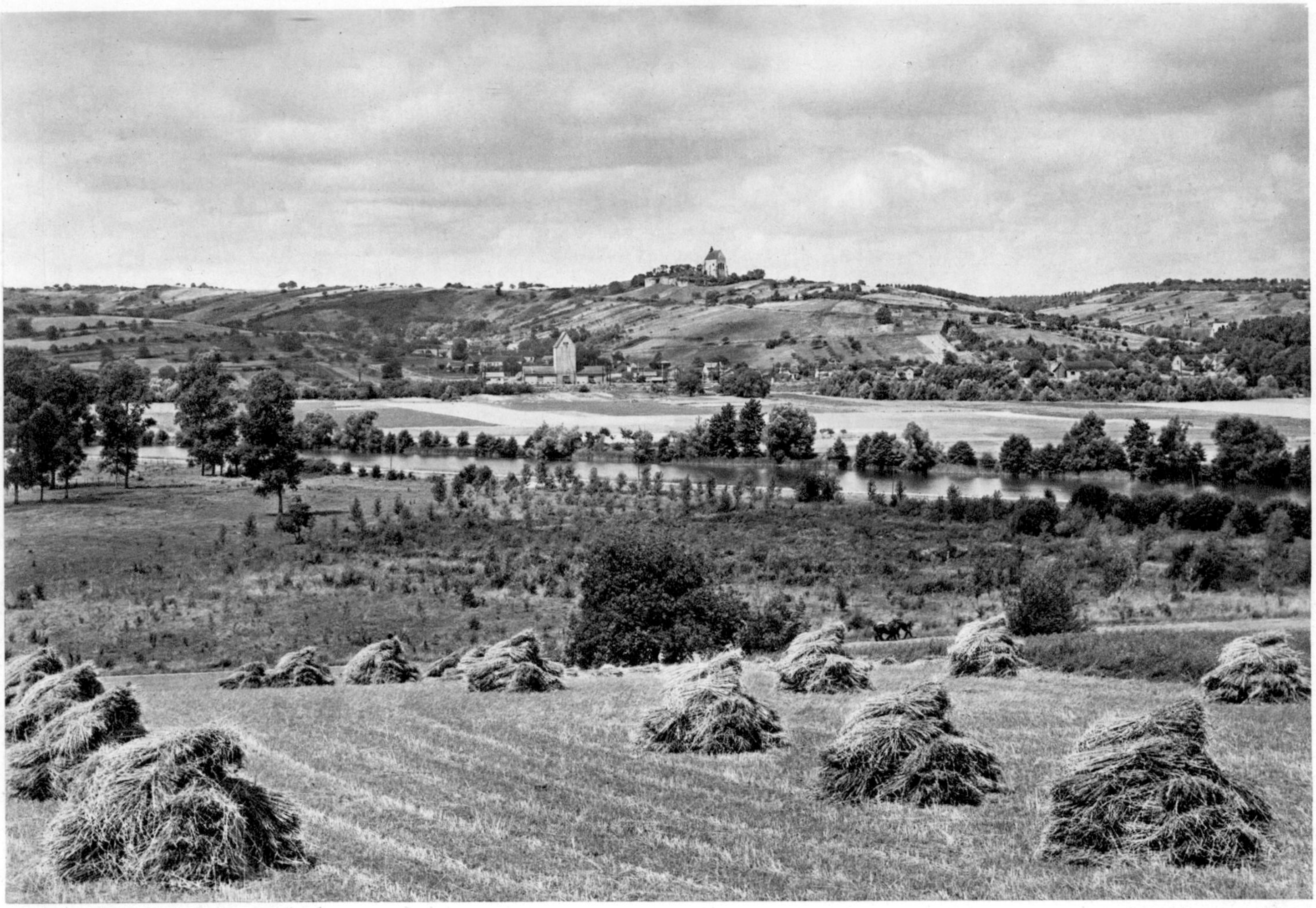

VALLÉE DE L'YONNE 26

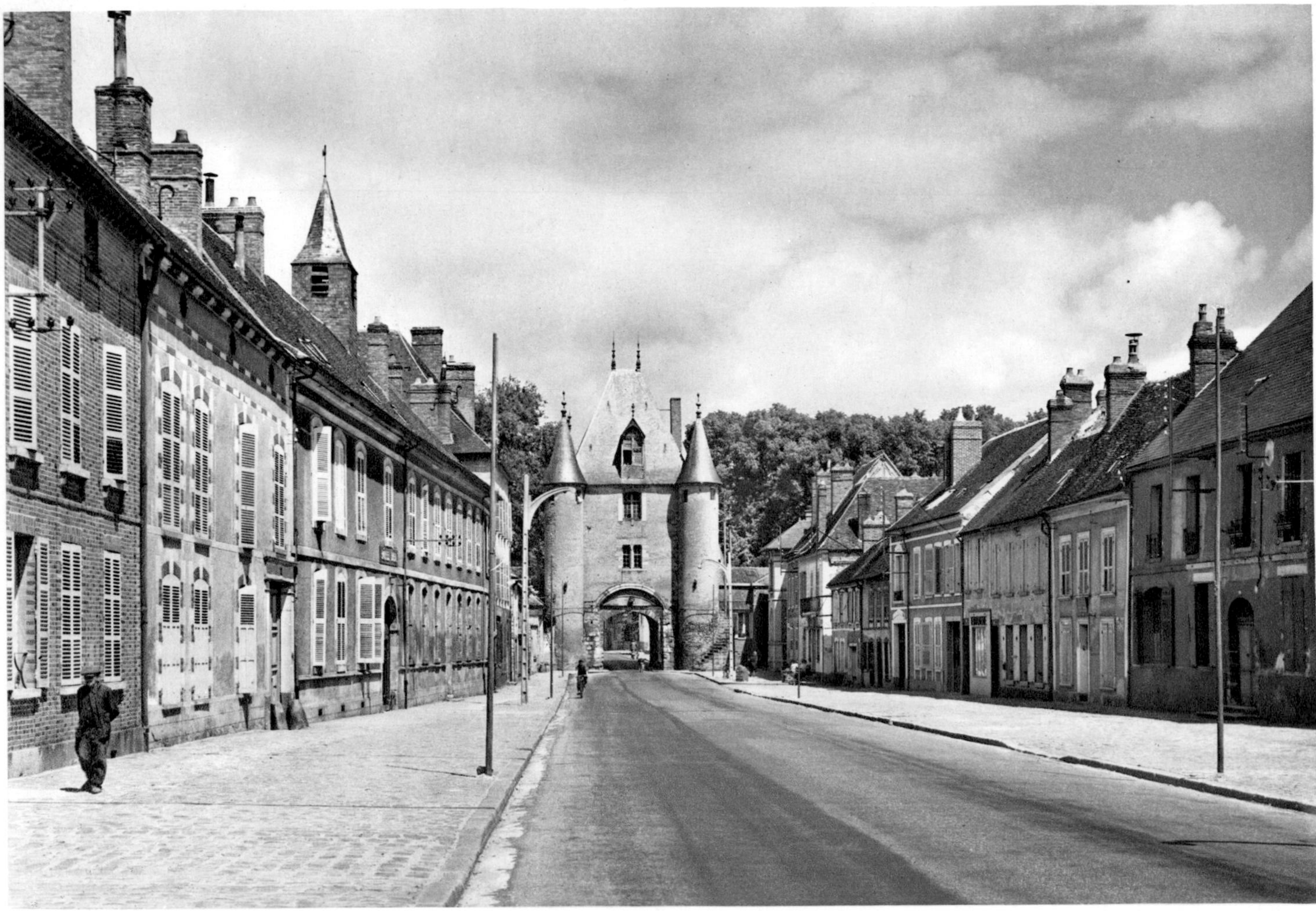

VILLENEUVE-SUR-L'YONNE 27

TROYES. ST-URBAIN

AUXERRE

CHABLIS

CHABLIS

AVALLON

VEZELAY. MADELEINE

AUTUN, PORTE D'ARROUX

SAINT-SEINE-L'ABBAYE 35

FERME EN BOURGOGNE 36

COTE D'OR

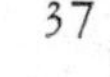

37

BEAUNE. HOTEL-DIEU

38

DIJON. PUITS DE MOISE

DÔLE

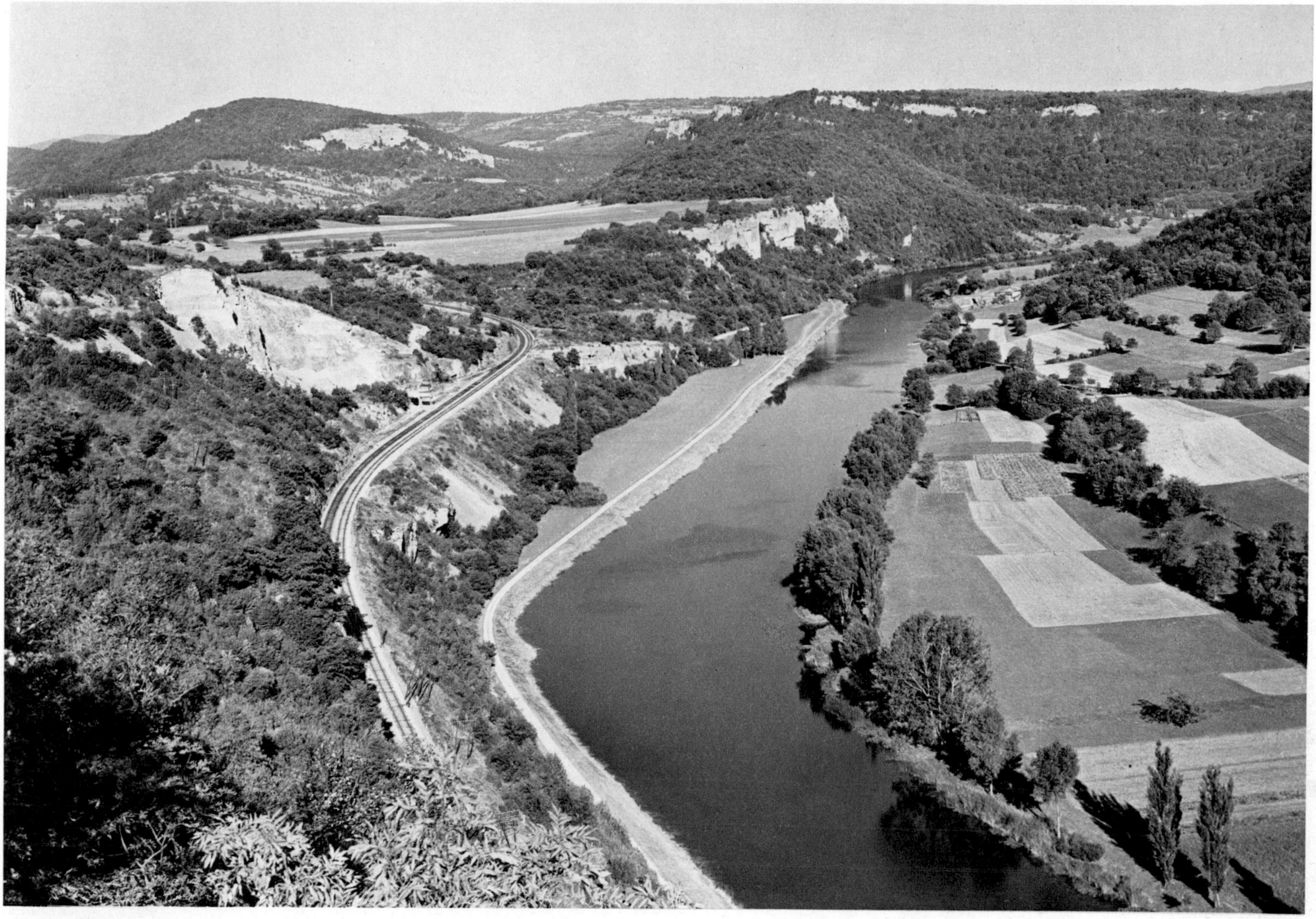

LE DOUBS

41

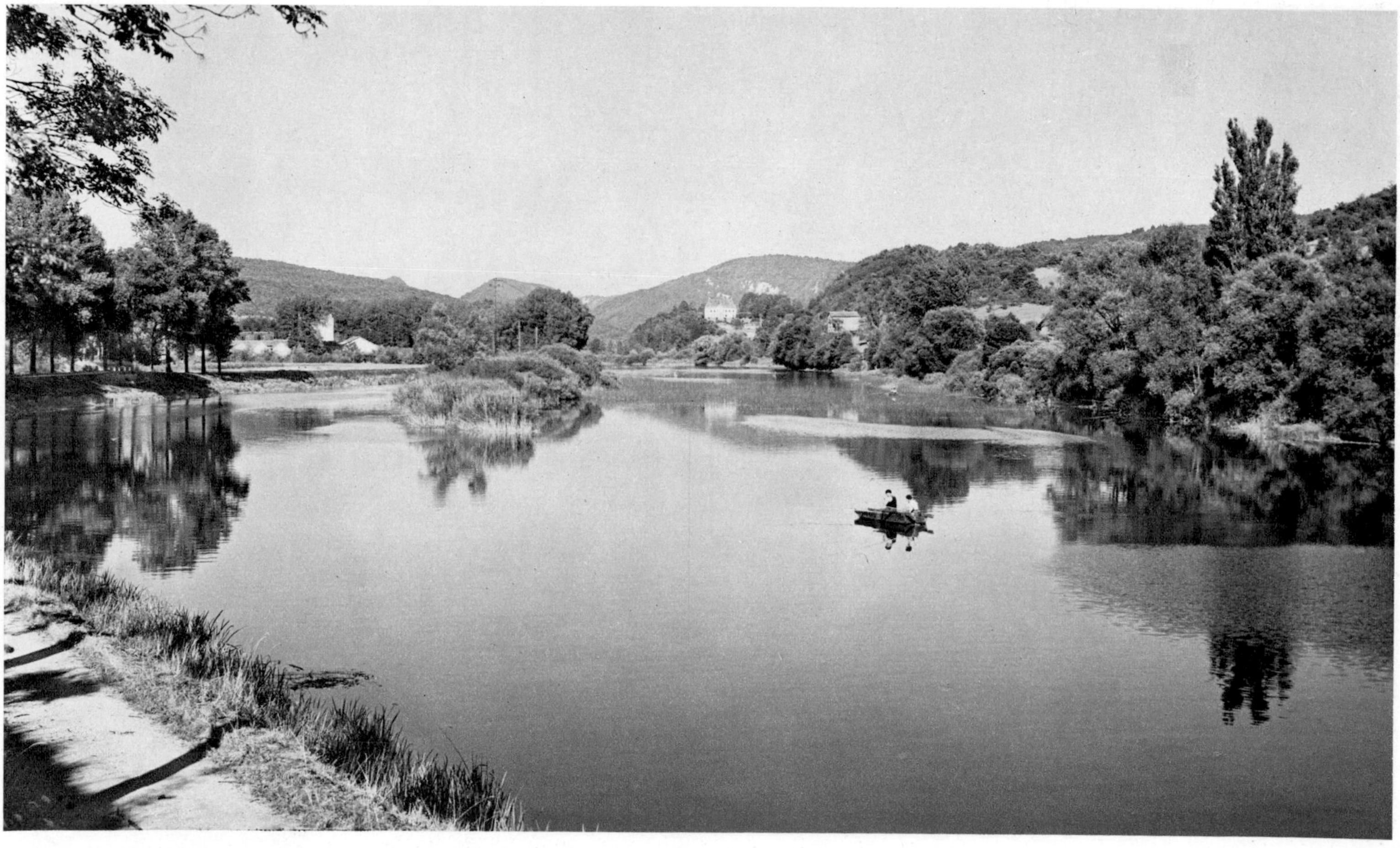

AUX BORDS DU DOUBS

42

ÉGLISE DE BROU. MAUSOLÉE DE MARGUERITE D'AUTRICHE

SALINS (JURA)

LYON. HOTEL DE VILLE

MACON

46

PONT ST-ESPRIT

47

VIENNE. ANCIENNE CATHÉDRALE ST-MAURICE

GRENOBLE

LE LAC LÉMAN A EVIAN

ANNECY

LA GRANDE CHARTREUSE

VALLÉE DE CHAMONIX

LE MONT BLANC

LA MER DE GLACE

BRIANÇON

EMBRUN

ROUTE NAPOLÉON

SISTERON

CASTELLANE

GRAND CAÑON DU VERDON

GRASSE

LA TURBIE

ANTIBES

CAP MARTIN

NICE. PROMENADE DES ANGLAIS 66

MENTON 67

MARSEILLE 68

SANARY-SUR-MER 69

CASSIS

TOUR GÉNOISE PRÈS DE BASTIA (CORSE)

AJACCIO

CALANCHE DE PIANA

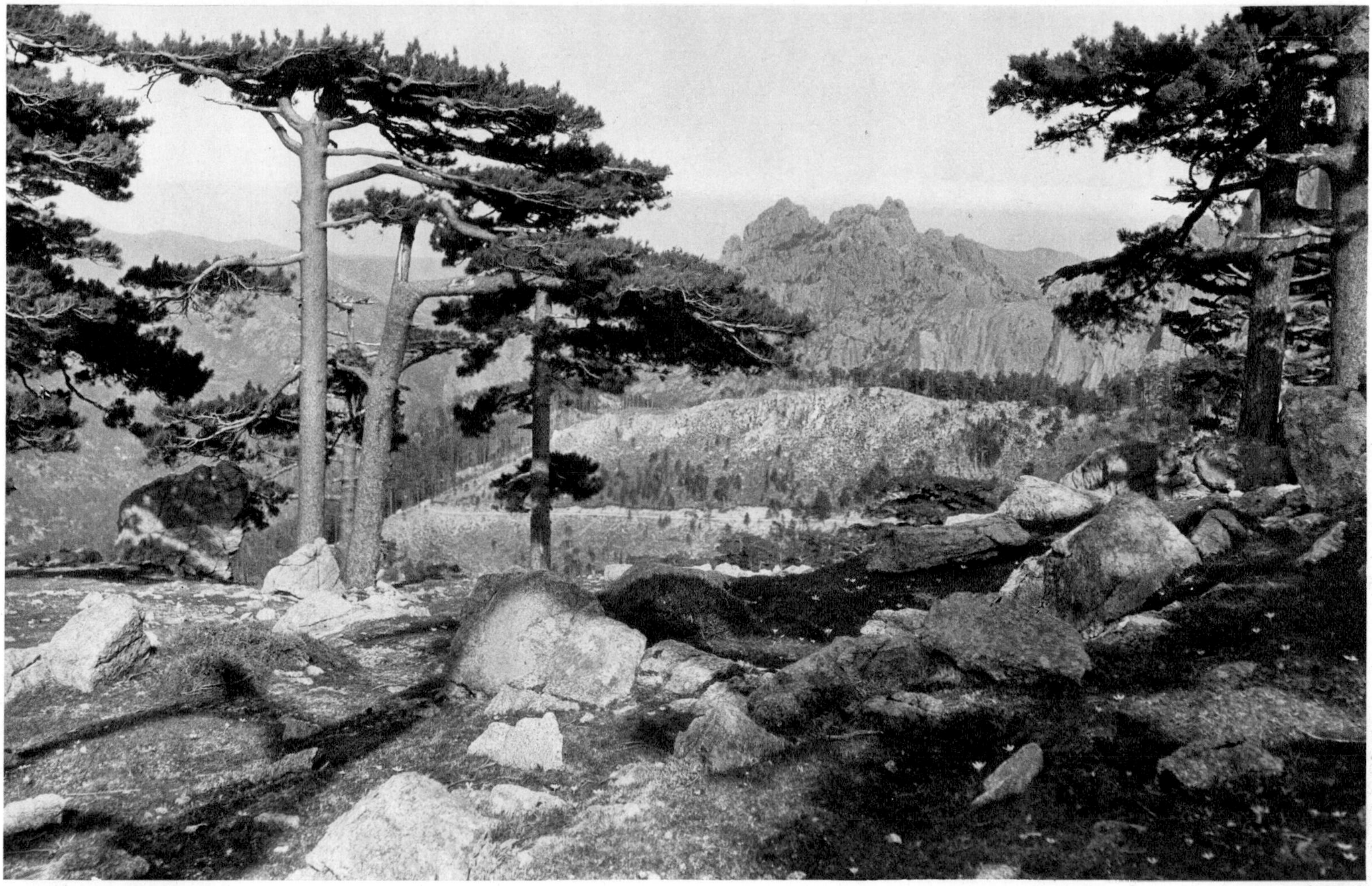

COL DE BAVELLA

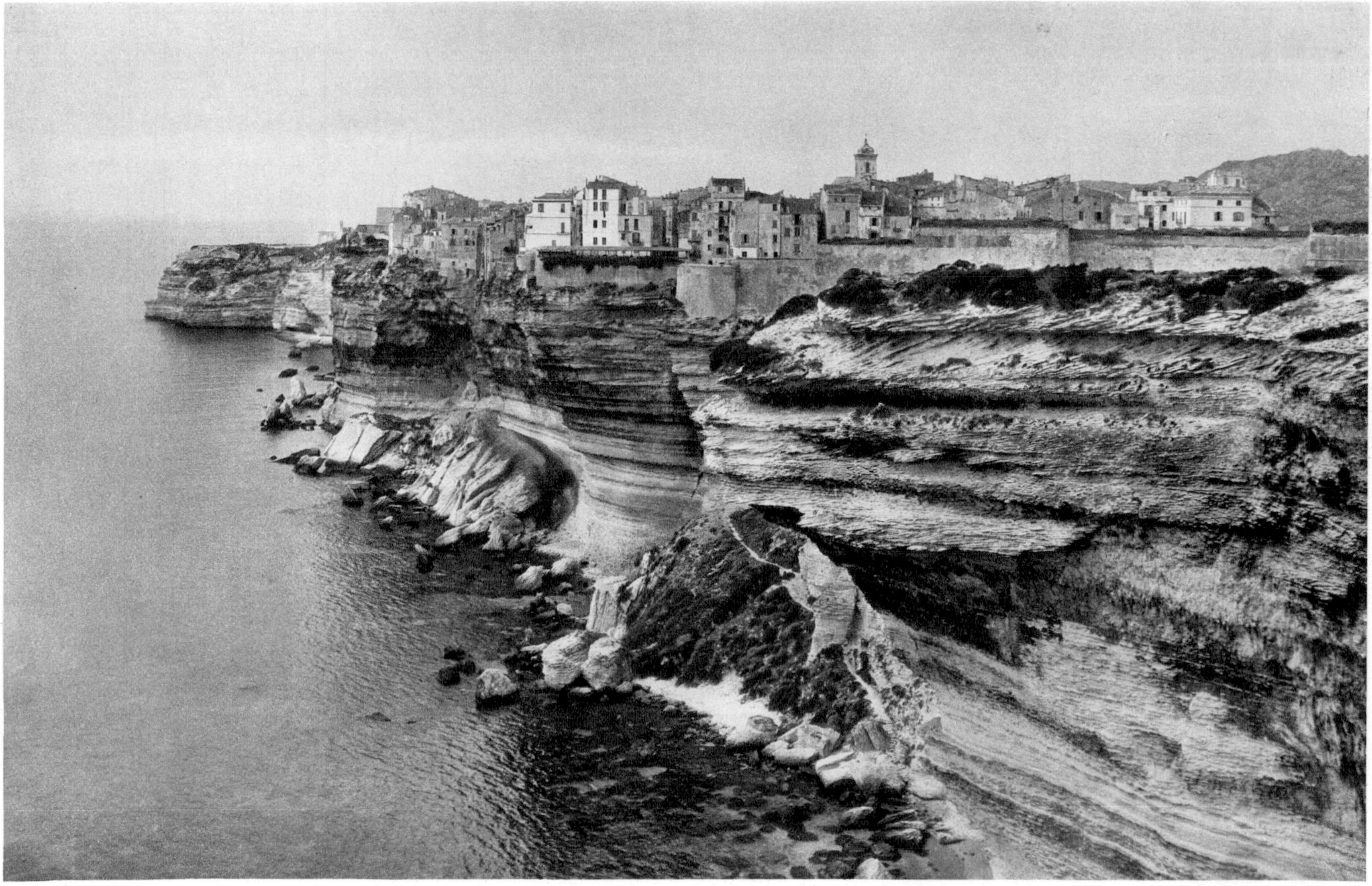

BONIFACIO

ERBALUNGA

BASTIA

LES BAUX

LES BAUX

ORANGE. ARC DE TRIOMPHE

80

ST-REMY (PROVENCE). LES ANTIQUES

81

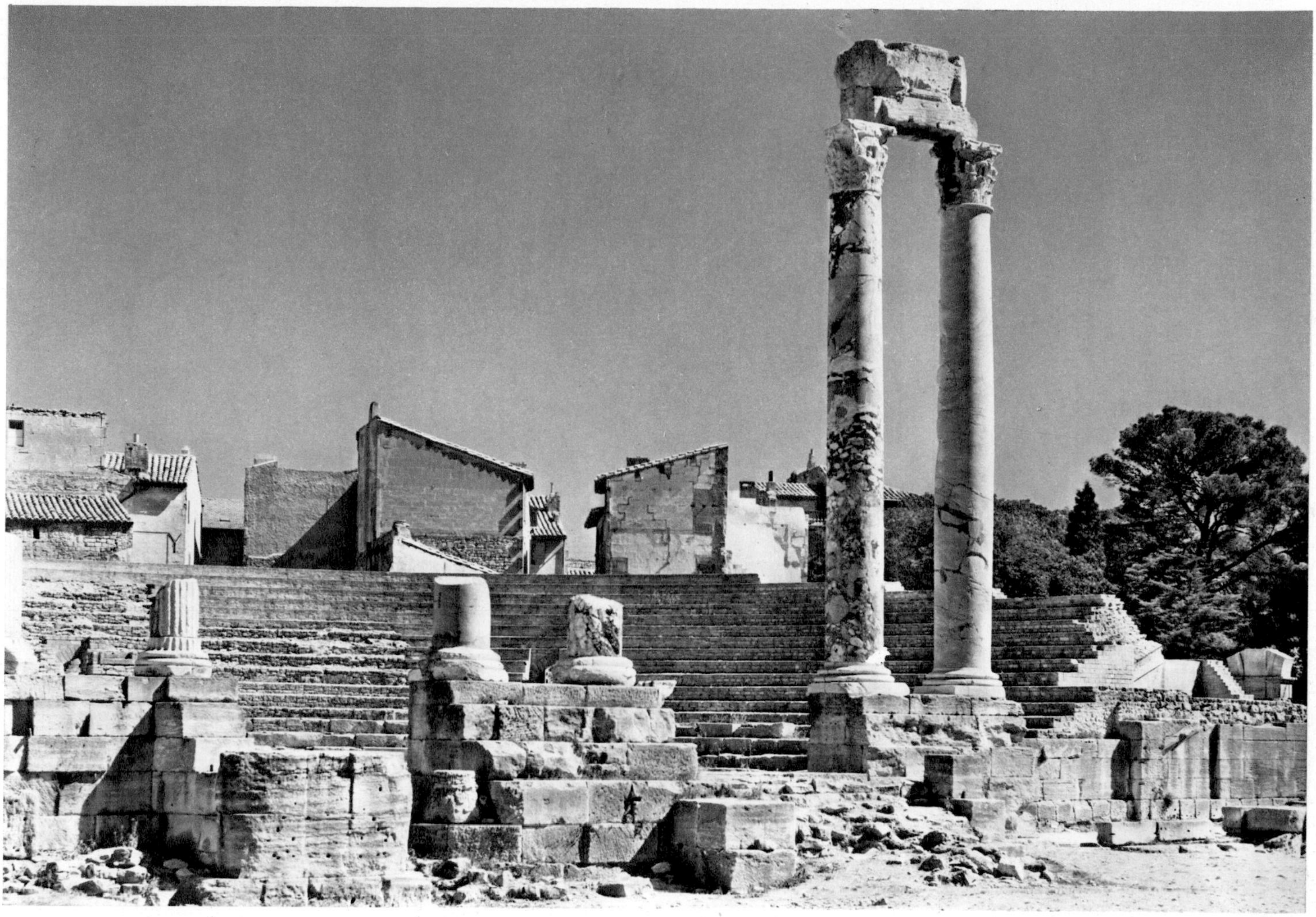

ARLES. THÉATRE ANTIQUE

82

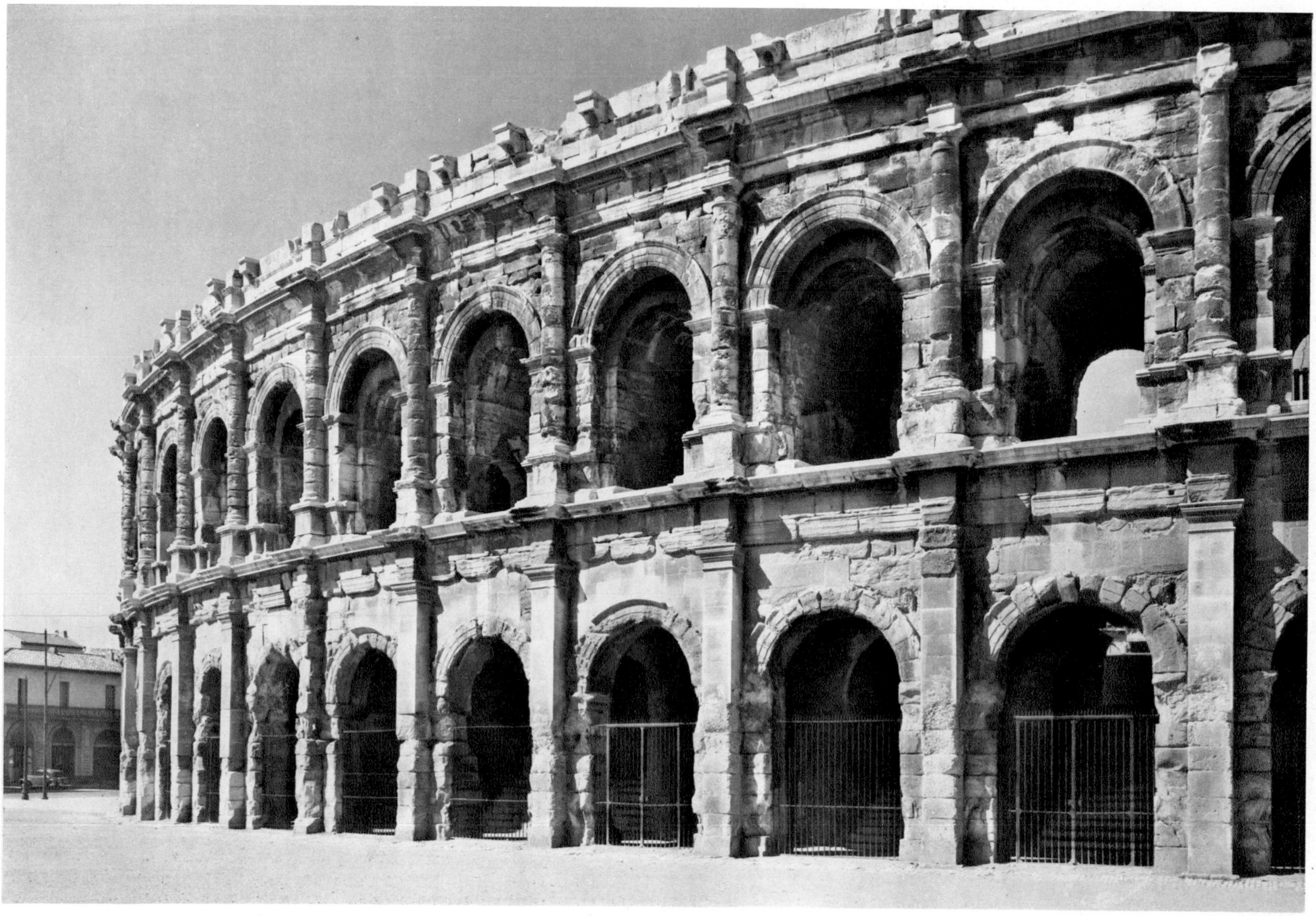

NIMES. ARÈNES

83

ARLES. LES ALISCAMPS

LE PONT DU GARD

AIX-EN-PROVENCE 86

ABBAYE DE MONTMAJOUR 87

CHATEAU DE TARASCON 88

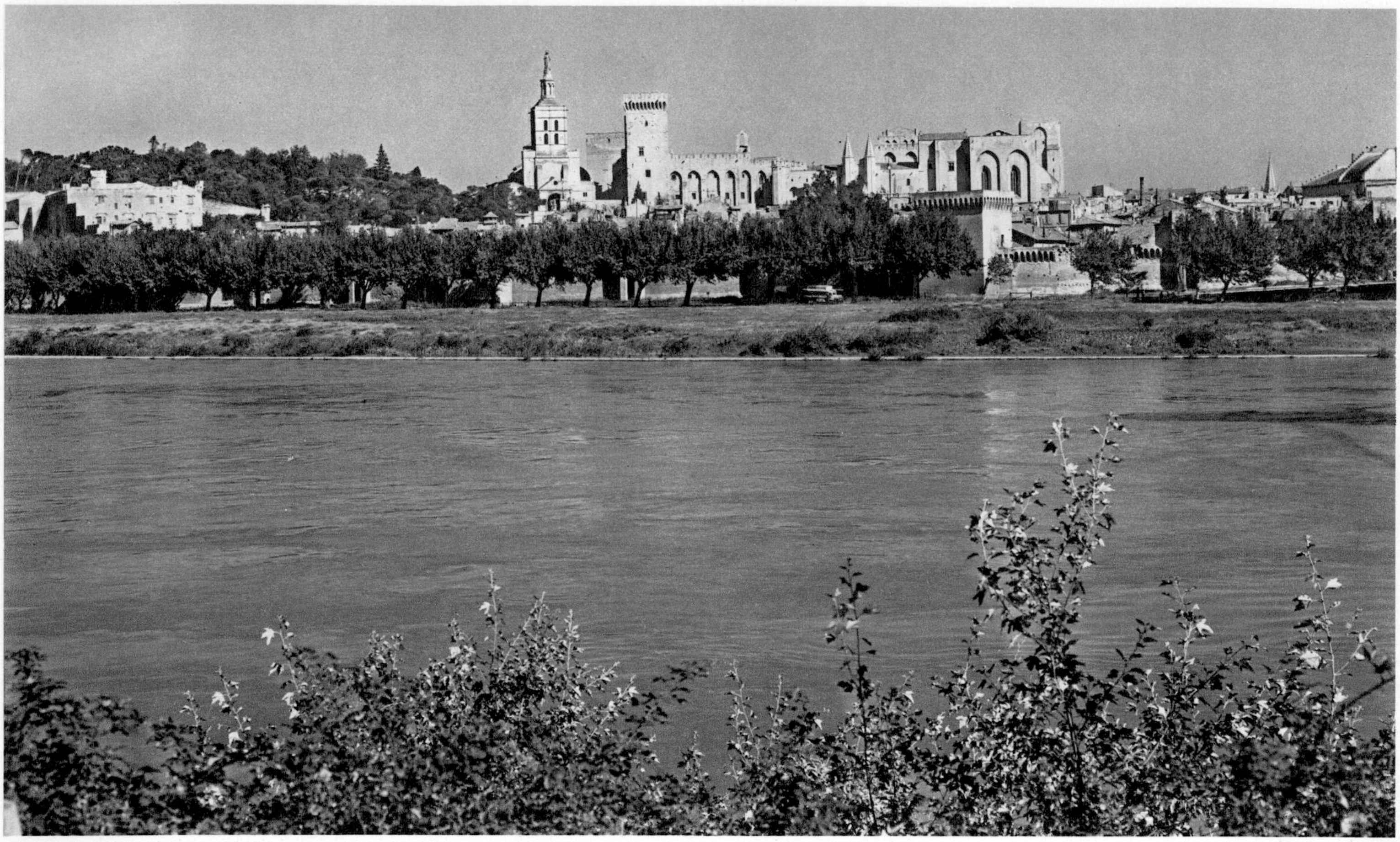

AVIGNON 89

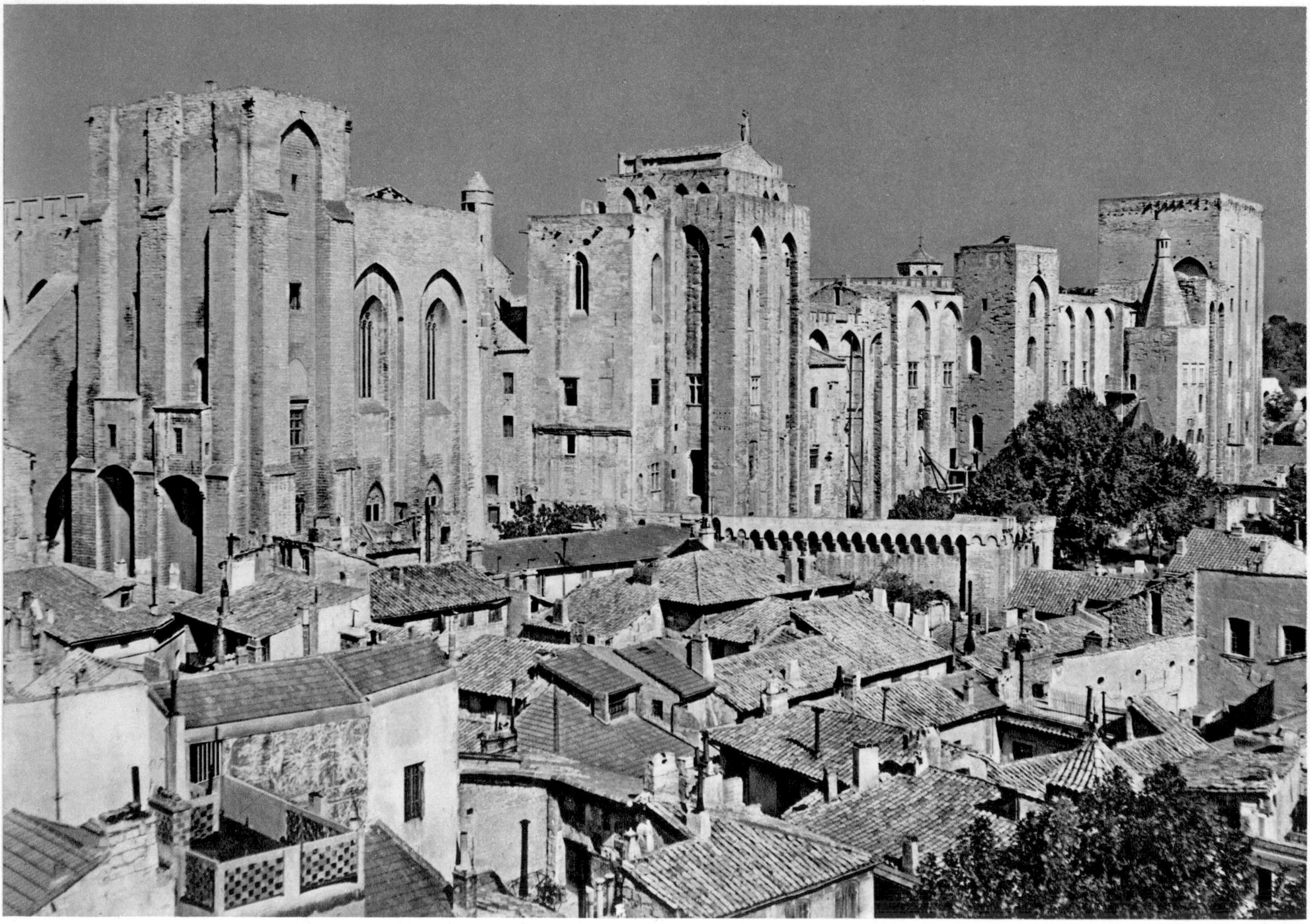

AVIGNON. PALAIS DES PAPES 90

AVIGNON. PALAIS DES PAPES

MARTIGUES

AIGUESMORTES

AIGUESMORTES 94

SAINT-GILLES 95

LA CATHÉDRALE D'AGDE

ELNE

BÉZIERS

PERPIGNAN

LE LITTORAL PRÈS DE BANYULS

100

BANYULS

101

COLLIOURE

FOIX

CIRQUE DE GAVARNIE

MUSCULDY 105

MONTRÉJEAU 106

CATHÉDRALE DE BAYONNE

CANAL PRÈS DE CERONS

CARCASSONNE

CARCASSONNE

FERME ALBIGEOISE

ALBI

MONTAUBAN. PONT DU TARN

113

CAHORS. PONT VALENTRÉ

114

TOULOUSE, HOTEL D'ASSÉZAT

MOISSAC

YSAIA

BORDEAUX. PLACE DES QUINCONCES

SAINT-ÉMILION

119

VIGNOBLES DU MÉDOC

120

VILLEFRANCHE-DE-ROUERGUE

CONQUES

SAINTE-ÉNIMIE

GORGES DU TARN

MILLAU 125

MILLAU 126

LES EYZIES-DE-TAYAC

LA ROCHELLE

LA ROCHELLE

PÉRIGUEUX 130

COGNAC 131

ANGOULÊME

LA CHAISE-DIEU

MURAT

LE PUY. ROCHER D'AIGUILLE

LE PUY

LAC DE GUÉRY (AUVERGNE) 137

LE MONT-DORE 138

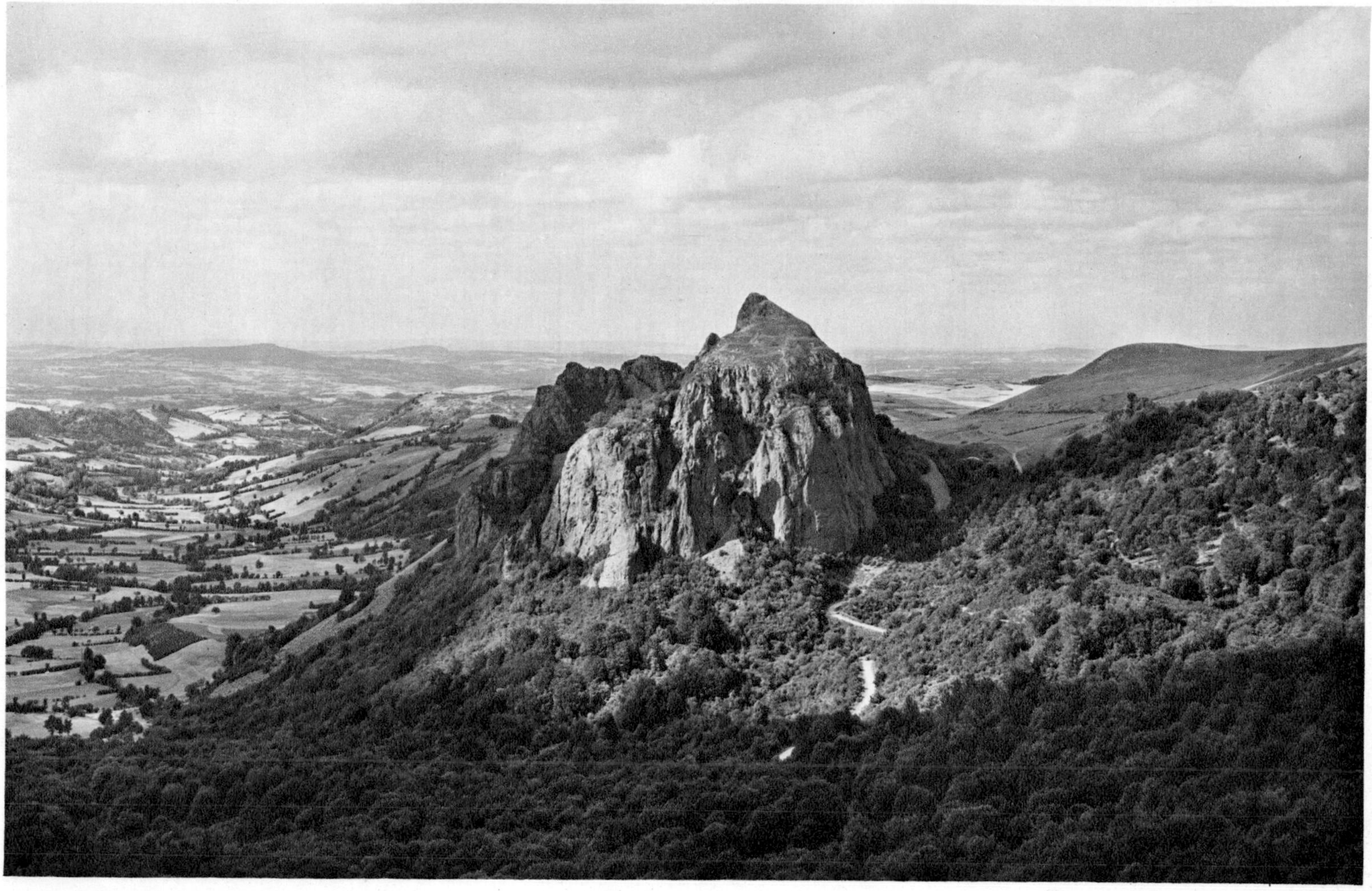

LE ROCHER SANADOIRE

139

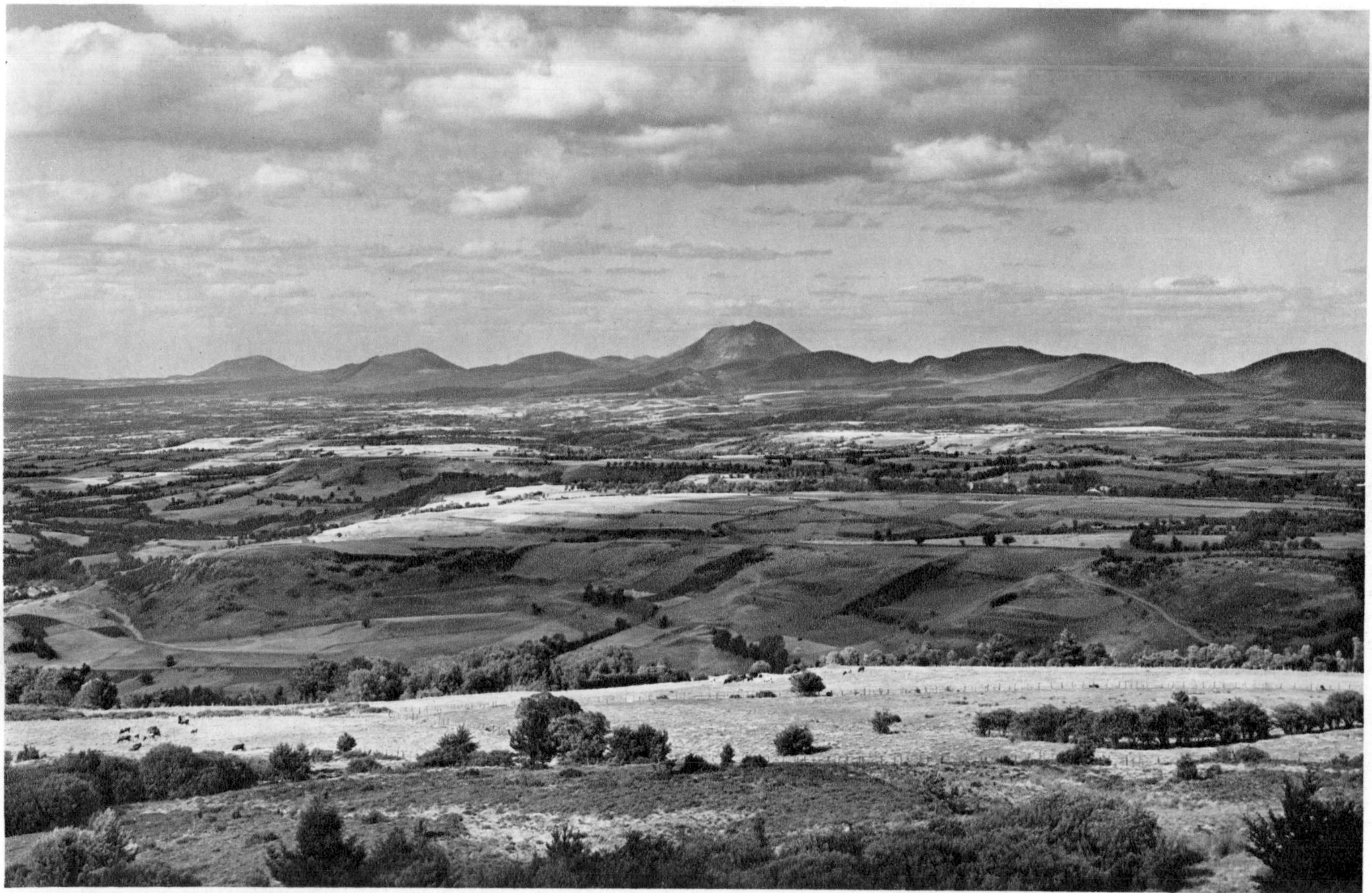

AUVERGNE. MONTS DÔMES

140

CATHÉDRALE DE MOULINS

CATHÉDRALE DE BOURGES

ST-BENOIT-SUR-LOIRE

CHATEAU DE SULLY-SUR-LOIRE

NEVERS. PALAIS DUCAL

ORLÉANS 146

GIEN 147

CHATEAU DE BLOIS

AMBOISE

CHATEAU DE CHAMBORD

150

CHATEAU DE CHAUMONT

151

CHATEAU DE CHEVERNEY

152

CHATEAU DE CHENONCEAU

153

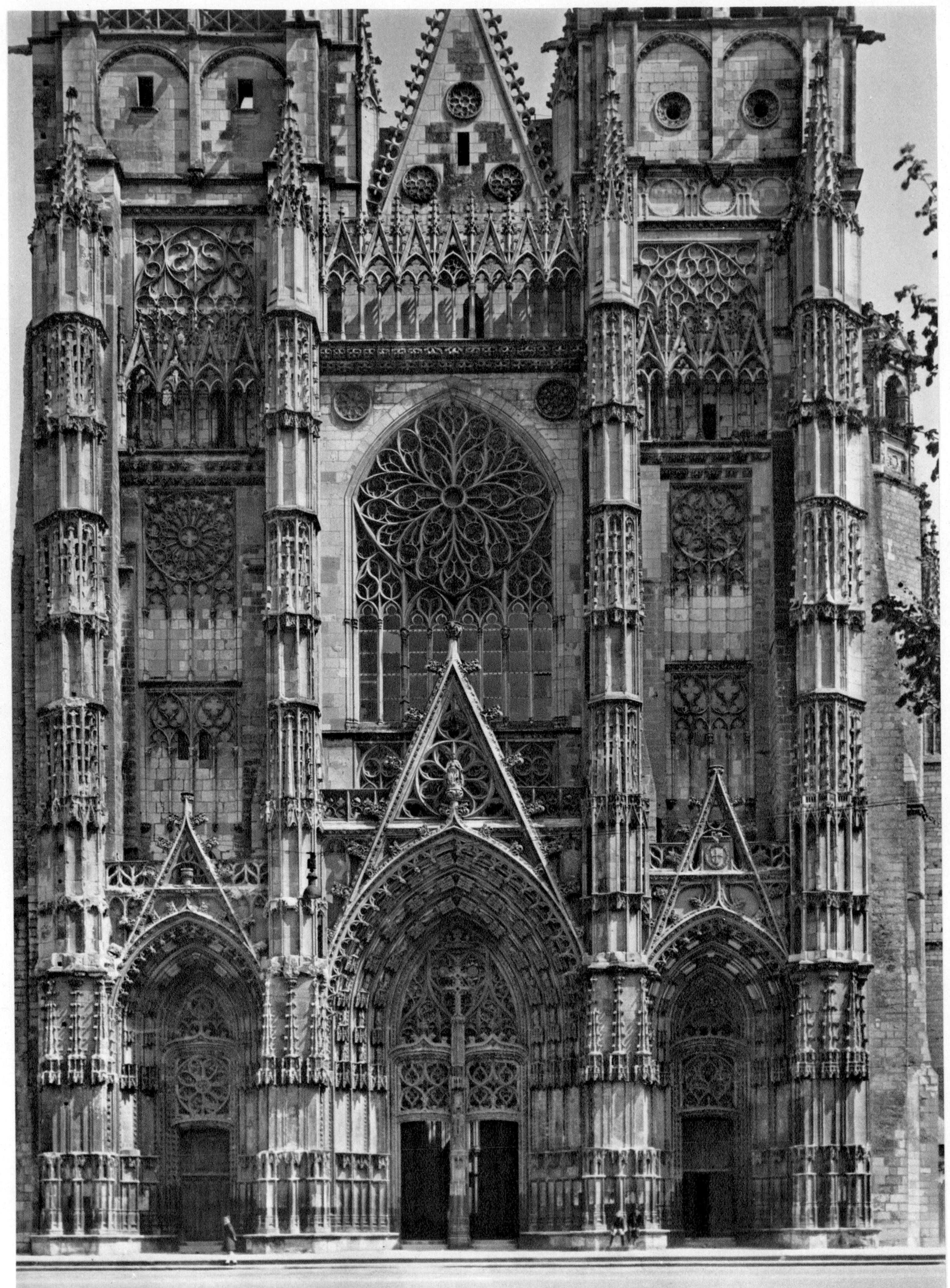

CATHÉDRALE DE TOURS

POITIERS. NOTRE-DAME-LA-GRANDE

CHINON. RUE VOLTAIRE

ABBAYE DE FONTEVRAULT

ST-SAVIN-SUR-GARTEMPE

ST-SAVIN-SUR-GARTEMPE

L'INDRE A REIGNAC

CHARTREUSE DU LIGET 161

ANGERS 162

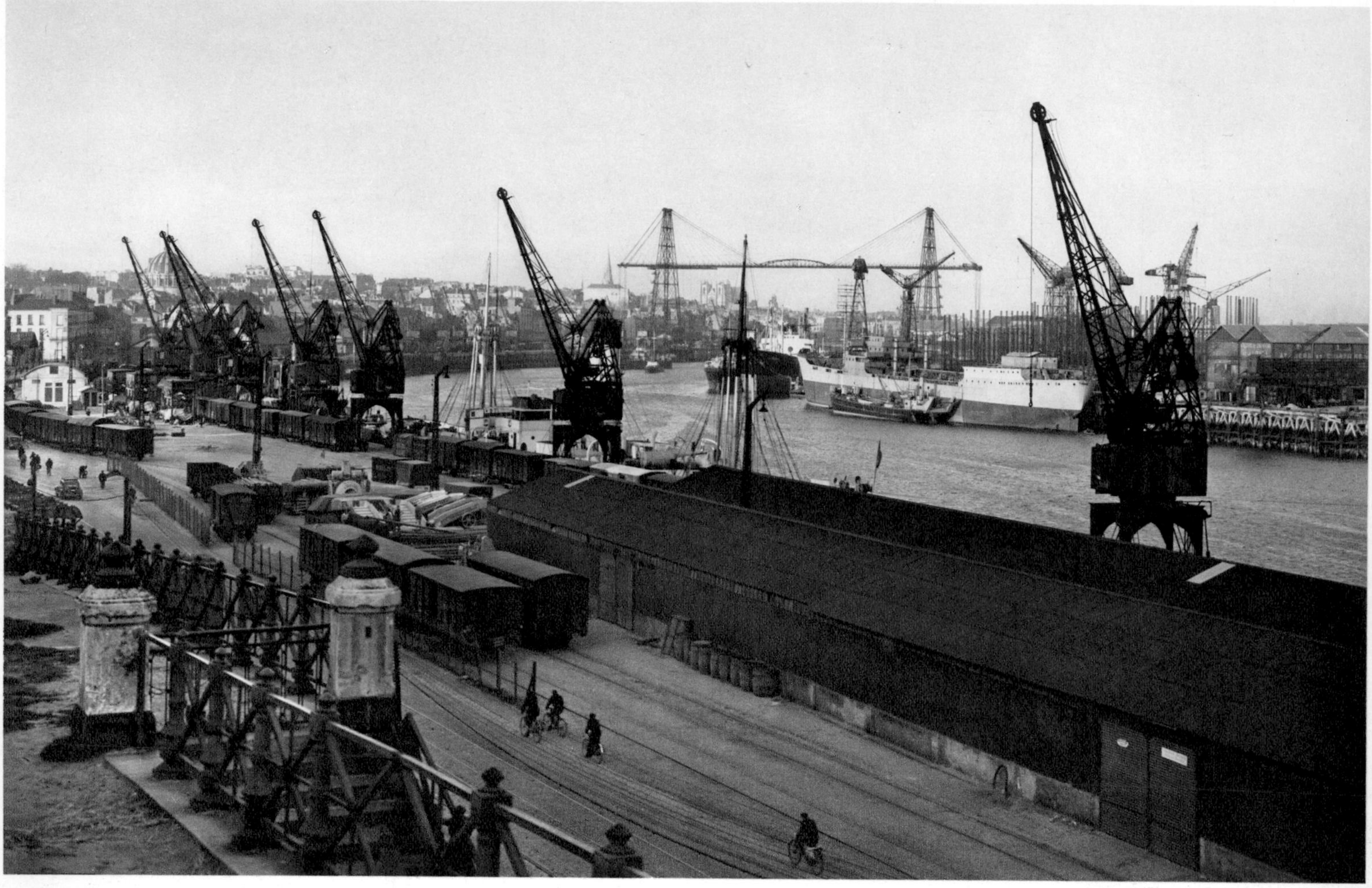

NANTES

163

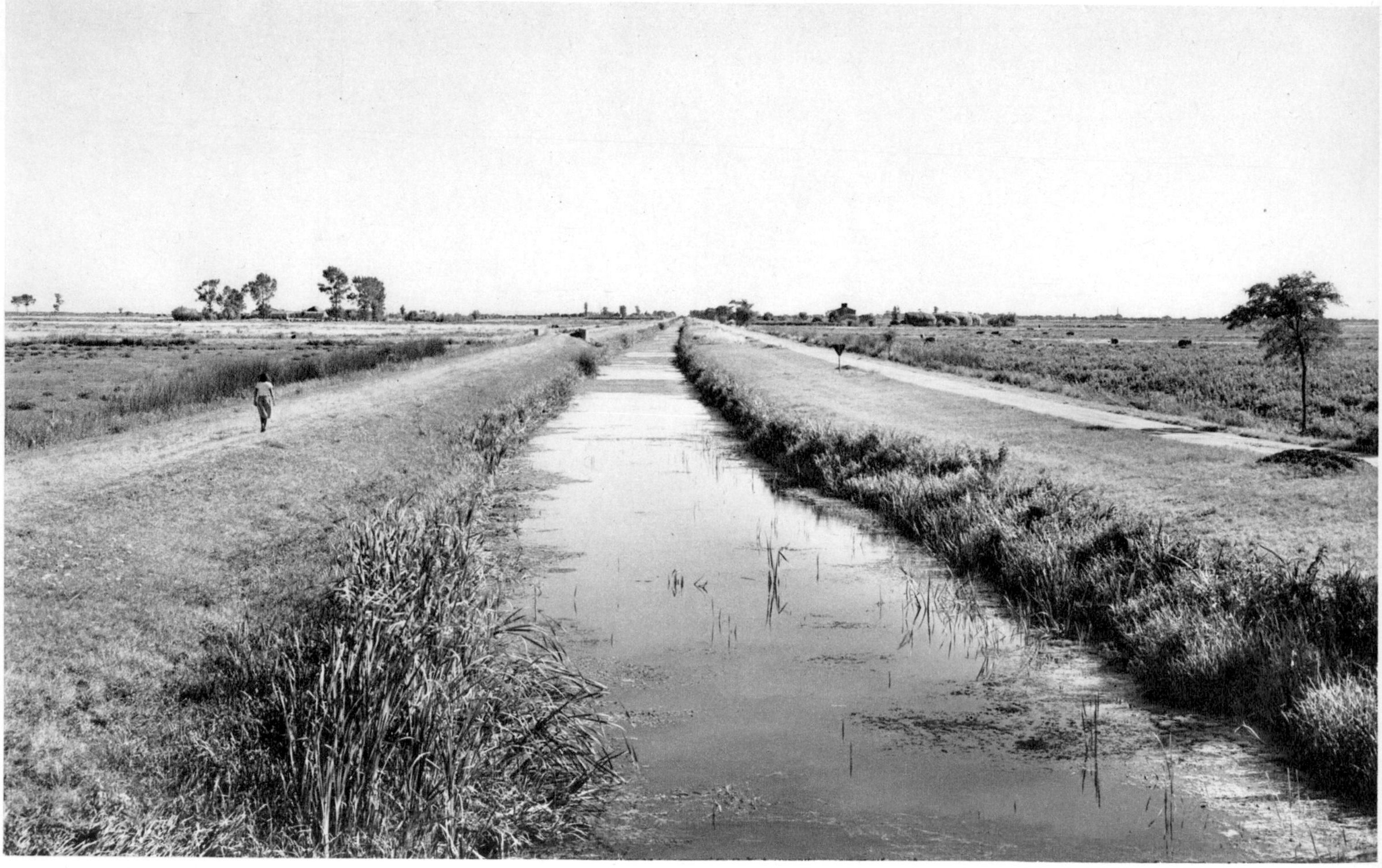

CANAL DU CLAIN (VENDÉE)

164

MORLAIX

VANNES

PARDON DE SAINTE-BARBE

167

LE CROISIC

168

CALVAIRE DE GUIMILIAU

CALVAIRE DE PLOUGASTEL-DAOULAS

CAP FRÉHEL 175

FORT LA LATTE 176

SAINT-MALO

DINAN

LE MONT SAINT-MICHEL

CATHÉDRALE DE BAYEUX

CATHÉDRALE DE COUTANCES

CAEN. ST-ETIENNE

CAEN. ST-PIERRE

ROUEN

HONFLEUR

MAISON RURALE NORMANDE

LE MANS

187

LAVAL

188

LOUVIERS. NOTRE-DAME

NOGENT-LE-ROTROU

CALAIS. MONUMENT DES BOURGEOIS DE CALAIS (RODIN)

ARRAS

ARRAS

ÉTRETAT

ABBEVILLE. ST-VULFRAN

CATHÉDRALE DE BEAUVAIS

BEAUVAIS. CATHÉDRALE ET PALAIS DE JUSTICE

CATHÉDRALE D'AMIENS

SOISSONS. ABBAYE DE ST-JEAN-DES-VIGNES

LAON

SENLIS

NOYON

REIMS. MONUMENT DE JEANNE D'ARC

REIMS

CANAL EN CHAMPAGNE

MEAUX

LANGRES

GUEBWILLER. ÉGLISE ST-LÉGER

NANCY. PLACE STANISLAS

DANS LES VOSGES

PAYSAGE JURASSIEN PRÈS DE BELFORT

RIQUEWIHR

SÉLESTAT. ÉGLISE ST-GEORGES

COLMAR. ANCIENNE DOUANE (KOIFHUS)

ZELLENBERG

STRASBOURG

HISTORICAL NOTES

1 The ROUTES NATIONALES, which radiate from Paris and traverse the whole country, are for the greater part lined with trees. They bear striking testimony to French centralism and the civilizing tradition taken over from the Romans. Following the creation by Henry IV of the office of *Grand-voyer* or Inspector of the King's Highway, the road network was further developed in a systematic manner for reasons of state; it played a very great part in promoting the prosperity and military strength of the Kingdom and, subsequently, of the Republic and the Empire. The many long straight stretches of road were eminently suited to further development for motor traffic. These roads are measured off by kilometre stones which indicate the distance from the Cathedral of Notre-Dame, the venerable centre of Old Paris.

2–10, 12 PARIS, the Gallic-Roman *Lutetia Parisiorum*, became in 505 the capital of Clovis the Merovingian, and from 987 onwards, the capital of the Capetians and thus of France. In modern times, because of the unique degree of centralization of the cultural life of the nation, it has played a leading part in moulding that of the entire world: as the home of painters, poets, the Press, revolutionaries, museums, centres of education, and fashion. The School of Notre-Dame and the University of Paris were famous throughout Europe even in the Middle Ages. Greater Paris has over five million inhabitants, of whom some 2,725,000 live in the city proper.

Close by the Seine, on the Field of Mars, the former Paris field for manœuvres, stands the 985-ft. high Eiffel Tower. This tremendous iron structure was built for the World Exhibition of 1889 by the firm of the engineer A. G. Eiffel, to the plans of the Swiss Maurice Koechlin, and although many artists and writers of the day, among them Verlaine, decried it as hideous, it became the popular symbol of modern Paris; it remained for decades the tallest building in the world, until it was surpassed by the highest skyscrapers of New York. From 1902 onwards the Eiffel Tower was used by Ferrié for radio experiments, and it has since served a new purpose as the frame for a huge aerial and as a broadcasting station.

3 Beyond the "quais" alongside the Seine, where the booksellers have set up their boxes on the walls, there rises the grey mass of NOTRE-DAME, the cathedral church of the Archbishop of Paris, with its impressive west front crowned with two squat towers—one of the earliest and most magnificent of Gothic creations. In the sixth century King Childebert erected on the city-island, upon the site of a Roman temple, the first Christian church. The present building was begun in 1163 under Bishop Maurice de Sully, a representation of whom appears in the tympanum of the right porch in the west front, and it was virtually completed around 1250 under Saint Louis.

4 At the PLACE DE LA CONCORDE the long axis extending from the Louvre and the Tuileries to the Arc de Triomphe intersects the transverse axis running from the Palais Bourbon, the seat of the National Assembly, to the church of the Madeleine. The view looking towards the Madeleine shows at the entrance to the Rue Royale two buildings by B. J. Gabriel, dating from the middle of the eighteenth century: on the left the Hotel Crillon and on the right the Ministry of Marine. The temple-like Madeleine building was started in 1764 but it took until 1826 to complete. During the French Revolution the Place de la Concorde became the place of execution, where Louis XVI, Marie Antoinette, Danton, Robespierre and 2,800 others fell victims to the guillotine. The present name originated in 1795 when the Terror was at an end. The square received its present form in the nineteenth century: in the centre there has stood since 1836 the obelisk from Luxor, which Mahommed Ali presented to the "people's king" Louis Philippe; beside it Hittorf erected two fountains modelled on those in St. Peter's Square in Rome.

5 The name LOUVRE was applied as early as the year 1200 to the castle which Philip Augustus built here around a great dungeon. The Renaissance king, Francis I, had the tower pulled down and a new royal palace built. Under his successors, and with the help of the leading architects of the country the palace was steadily extended. Louis XIV decided against a grandiose Baroque scheme of the Cavaliere Bernini and in favour of a design of the native school, better suited to the *genius loci*; the "Colonnade", inspired by Vitruvius, which forms the eastern façade of the Louvre, is the work of the talented physician and amateur architect Claude Perrault.

In the year 1680, when the work on the new Louvre

was still unfinished, the Court moved to Versailles, and the Louvre was neglected until Napoleon I gave it fresh lustre, after it had been turned into a museum in 1793. He had works of art brought from conquered countries and so made the Louvre the richest museum in the world. Although in 1815 the Allies took back the property which had been stolen from them, the collection was steadily enriched in the nineteenth century and it has preserved its reputation up to the present day.

6 THE INVALIDES. With its slender, gilded dome the Church of Les Invalides forms the brilliant centre piece of the south front of the Hôtel des Invalides. In 1671 Louis XIV ordered the construction of a large complex of buildings which were intended to provide accommodation for up to 7,000 invalid pensioner soldiers, and in 1679 the "Roi Soleil" commanded his leading architect, Jules Hardouin-Mansart, to add a church which was to be a worthy memorial of his glorious reign. The church is one of the masterpieces of the "classical" style by which French Baroque distinguishes itself from its contemporary counterparts in other European countries. The interior was altered between 1843 and 1861 to provide a tomb for Napoleon I, whose remains were brought to Paris from St. Helena in 1840.

7 The ISLE SAINT-LOUIS between two arms of the Seine forms, together with the Isle de la Cité, the heart of Old Paris. It is a quiet little town in itself, with distinguished private houses dating from the seventeenth century.

8 From 1578, when Henry III had the Pont Neuf built, onwards the French continued through succeeding centuries to confirm their reputation as bridge builders by constructing additional stone bridges over the Seine. The PONT ROYAL was built between 1685 and 1689 by P. Romain and J. Gabriel according to plans by Mansart, in place of the earlier wooden bridge.
On the right bank of the Seine stands the PAVILLON DE FLORE, which belonged to the Tuileries Palace, and now forms the south-west corner of the Louvre and the end of the grand gallery. The building was given its present aspect by Lefuel, under Napoleon III, and contained the apartments of the Empress Eugénie.

9 The building of the FONDATION SUISSE of the CITÉ UNIVERSITAIRE of Paris is one of the representative works of the architect Le Corbusier and of the architectural style he represents. This style is free from traditional associations and has developed in accordance with the possibilities afforded by modern technique. The southern façade of this cubic concrete construction resting on pillars is completely taken up by the huge windows.
The Cité Universitaire, with its buildings respesentative of the widest range of styles and nationalities, was founded in 1920 so as to make available to the students of the famous Paris colleges in the overcrowded city, accommodation which would meet modern hygienic requirements.

10 The PALAIS DES MUSÉES D'ART MODERNE was created for the great exhibition of 1937. The two wings, in which the French State and the City of Paris display their collections of modern art, are linked by a colonnade (our picture shows the south aspect facing the Seine). The architects were Dondel, Aubert, Viard and Dastugue; the large bas-relief is by Janniot.

11 The church of LE RAINCY, a village situated six miles to the east of Paris, was built between 1920 and 1924 and, with its use of reinforced concrete and glass, is one of the pioneer creations of the architect Auguste Perret.

12 SAINT-GERMAIN-DES-PRÉS is the oldest church in Paris. It was built in the eleventh century as part of a great abbey, at the place where, in the sixth century, the Merovingian Childebert, acting at the instigation of St. Germanus, Bishop of Paris, had erected the first church. The lower part of the tower was already in existence in 1014, the upper part was added in the twelfth century.
The Place St. Germain with its cafés is a focal point of that quarter on the left bank of the Seine which is the haunt of artists and writers: it has acquired some reputation as the meeting place of the Existentialists or whatever intellectual coterie happens to be in vogue.

13–14 The Palace of CHANTILLY, which the Connetable Anne de Montmorency had built by Jean Bullant about 1560, stands in the middle of a lake. That part of the original castle which is still preserved is called the Capitainerie or the Petit Château, to distinguish it from the Grand Château lying behind it; the latter was added in the nineteenth century. The Connetable established his magnificent library, which is still intact, during his seven-year banishment here and kept himself occupied as patron of the fine arts. In the following century the great Condé had Le Nôtre, the garden architect of Louis XIV, lay out the park. The Duke of Aumale, who inherited the seat from the Condés, removed all traces of the devastation wrought by the Revolution and rebuilt the great palace entirely anew. In 1886 he presented the entire estate with its unique collections to the Institut de France, of which he was a member. The Condé Museum in the palace is particularly rich in precious miniatures, drawings, paintings, medallions and other specimens of the smaller art forms.

15–17 From 1682, when Louis XIV established his residence there, up to the Revolution of 1789 the Palace of VERSAILLES remained almost without interruption the seat of the kings of France. With its brilliant court ceremonies Versailles was for a whole century the unsurpassed model for the other princely courts of Europe. Le Vau enlarged the hunting lodge of Louis XIII to meet the new requirements; Hardouin-Mansart then added as a brilliant end-piece to the park designed by Le Nôtre the garden façade glistening with marble, containing 375 windows, and extending for the then enormous width of 634 yards. In the projecting central section (Ill. 16) there is the Hall of Mirrors, where the German Empire was proclaimed in 1871 and the Peace Conference sat in 1919.

The interior furnishing and decoration of the palace with its fabulous display of magnificence, which is nevertheless always kept within the confines of good taste and dignity, is predominantly the work of Charles Le Brun. The SALON DE LA GUERRE (1678, Ill. 15) contains a relief by Coysevox depicting Louis XIV on horseback; this is set among decoration consisting of various kinds of marble, wrought bronze and gilt stucco.

Plate 17 shows the Fountain of Diana and the Avenue of the Three Fountains on the north side of the garden terrace in front of the palace.

18 Louis XIV had the GRAND TRIANON of Versailles built by Hardouin-Mansart in 1687 in place of the earlier "Trianon de Porcelaine", so that he might from time to time recuperate there from his official engagements in the great palace. The two parts of the single-storey building, the walls of which are faced with white and pink marble, are connected by an open colonnade, the pillars and pilasters of which are of green and pink marble.

19 The Palace of RAMBOUILLET (Seine-et-Oise) was frequently used by the kings of France as a hunting lodge; Francis I died here in 1547. The park, which merges into the forest of Rambouillet, and its canals, are in the main the work of Fleurian d'Armenouville, who acquired the palace in 1700 but had to yield it soon afterwards to the Count of Toulouse, a natural son of Louis XIV. Louis XIV finally turned it into a royal estate. Since the presidency of Élie Faure (1896), the Presidents of the French Republic have been in the habit of spending part of the summer here.

20–21 FONTAINEBLEAU (Seine-et-Marne) developed from a small hunting estate of the kings of France, situated in the middle of the forest of Bière. Francis I caused a magnificent Renaissance palace to be built in place of the castle of his predecessors, and the work started in 1527 under Giles Le Breton. Under Henry II it was decorated by Italian artists, and his successors, in particular Henry IV, added further buildings. Napoleon restored the entire palace and grounds and it was one of his favourite residences.

In the COUR DU CHEVAL BLANC or COUR DES ADIEUX (Ill. 20) Napoleon bade farewell to his Guards on the morning of 20th April, 1814, following the signing of his abdication on 7th April. The main west façade of the palace with its five "pavilions" has been extensively renovated since the time of Francis I. The double, horseshoe-shaped staircase in the centre was the work of Jean Ducerceau (1634).

The SALLE DU CONSEIL (Ill. 21) was built under Francis I; its furnishing (1753), however, is one of the finest examples of the style of Louis XV, in whose reign French decorative art reached its highest pitch of refinement. The paintings are by F. Boucher, C. Van Loo and others; the chairs are upholstered with Beauvais tapestries.

22 The royal palace of COMPIÈGNE (Oise) evolved, as did that of Fontainebleau, from a hunting seat. Louis XIV

said: "In Versailles I live like a king, in Fontainebleau like a nobleman and in Compiègne like a peasant." Louis XV, employing the architects Gabriel, father and son, replaced the old palace with a new one begun in 1738. The apartments, which were ransacked during the Revolution, were magnificently decorated and furnished anew under Napoleon. It was here that the Emperor in 1810 presented to the Court his second wife, Marie-Louise of Austria. Under Napoleon III and the Empress Eugénie the palace of Compiègne once again enjoyed a period of great social brilliance. The library of Napoleon I is a good example of the Empire style of 1810; the furniture is by Jacob; the bookcases which cover the walls are made of cashew wood.

23–24 On a hill in the rich and fruitful district of Beauce lies the old cathedral town of CHARTRES (Eure-et-Loir), the Roman *Autricum*, dominated by its cathedral. With the introduction of Christianity into Gaul in the fourth century, the original church was established on the site where heathen rites had been practised. The growing power of attraction of the image of Our Lady at Chartres encouraged the building of ever larger edifices, following successive conflagrations. With the harmony of its architecture, the wealth and spiritual content of its sculpture and the magnificence of its stained glass, the Early Gothic cathedral church, begun in 1194, bears in unique fashion the imprint of the entire range of mediaeval art dedicated to the glory of God. Plate 23 shows the south-west corner, with an angel of the twelfth century; the sundial was added in the sixteenth century.

25 BEAUCE, with its broad cornfields is called the granary of France and is agriculturally one of the richest parts of the country.

26 In the valley of the YONNE, a tributary of the Seine, between Joigny and Sens.

27 The little town of VILLENEUVE-SUR-YONNE (Yonne) was established by Louis VII (Louis le Jeune) in 1163, and laid out on a regular plan. The main street has the gates of the mediaeval fortified town at each end.

28 TROYES (Aube) has 60,000 inhabitants and was once the capital of Champagne. It possesses in addition to its cathedral a number of other churches which bear witness to its importance and wealth, particularly towards the end of the Middle Ages. The Church of St. Urban was founded in 1262 by Pope Urban IV on the site of the cobbler's workshop of his father. The wall area is almost entirely broken up by large windows, giving the structure its air of brightness which anticipates a later age.

29 AUXERRE, chief town of the Departement Yonne, stands on the left bank of the Yonne, and the former cathedral of Saint-Etienne towers above it. The church dates back to the fourth century; between the thirteenth and sixteenth centuries it was rebuilt a second time in the Gothic style of the Champagne.

30–31 CHABLIS (Yonne) is the centre of the wine district of Lower Burgundy, where the white "Chablis" is produced. Ill. 30 shows a view from a vineyard looking towards the little town and the tower of the church of St. Martin, which dates from the twelfth century; Ill. 31 is of a mill on the fringe of the town.

32 AVALLON (Yonne). The view from the Place St. Lazare looking along the old-world Rue Bocquillot towards the Tour de l'Horloge (fifteenth century).

33 VÉZELAY (Yonne) is the seat of a Benedictine abbey founded in the ninth century. The acquisition of the relics of St. Magdalene made the Madeleine abbey church the goal of innumerable mediaeval pilgrims. It was here that Bernard of Clairvaux summoned people to join the Second Crusade, and the kings Philip Augustus of France and Richard Cœur de Lion took up the cross. The basilica erected in the eleventh century is one of the finest Romanesque churches in France. The porch, leading from the narthex to the central nave, is decorated with a richly sculptured tympanum which represents Christ imbuing the Apostles with the Holy Spirit.

34 AUTUN (Saône-et-Loire), the ancient *Augustodunum*, was one of the most important towns of old Gaul; under Augustus it superseded Bibracte as the capital of the Aedui. Various ancient monuments, among them the Porte d'Arroux illustrated here, show that at the time of the Romans the town was of about twice its present extent. Its wealth brought upon it in the course

of the centuries attacks and sackings by the Alemanni, the Huns, Burgundians, Saracens, Normans and finally the English. The Counts of Autun became in 880 Dukes of Burgundy, and resided here as such until 1276.

35 SAINT-SEINE-L'ABBAYE (Côte-d'Or). Here at the south-west extremity of the plateau of Langres, beside a minor tributary of the Saône, not far from the source of the Seine, St. Sequanus (St. Seine) founded a monastery in the year 534. Its church, which dates from the thirteenth to the fifteenth centuries, forms the centre of the present-day village.

36 A farm in BURGUNDY.

37 Vineyards of the CÔTE-D'OR. Between Dijon and Macon on the right bank of the Saône the broad and fertile Burgundian plain is bordered by the hills of the Côte-d'Or, formerly called the Pays de la Montagne. Here, on the chalky soil round about the old wine centre of Beaune, grow the famous wines of Burgundy, most of them red wines such as Chambertin, Nuits-Saint-Georges, Pommard and Volnay. The vine stocks "pineau" and "noirien", in particular, yield the rich red wine of this region.
The wines of Burgundy were famous even in mediaeval times. An edict of Charles VI, dated 1415—the oldest of its kind—already distinguishes between the wines of Lower Burgundy (in particular the white wines of Chablis) and the wines of Upper Burgundy —the Beaune of the Côte-d'Or, and the produce of Macon, which includes Beaujolais, of Tournus and of Dijon.

38 BEAUNE (Côte-d'Or), the Roman *Belna*, was the principal town of a Burgundian county which Louis XI incorporated in the Kingdom of France in the fifteenth century. The Gothic hospital (Hôtel-Dieu) founded in 1443 by Nicolas Robin, Chancellor of Burgundy, is built in the Flemish style, partly in wood. The sisters still wear the large white winged head-dress which recalls their Flemish origin. The hospital is supported mainly by the proceeds of the vineyards which belong to it.

39 DIJON (Côte-d'Or) is now a town of 100,000 inhabitants. The *Divio* of ancient times, it belonged from 1015 onwards to the Duchy of Burgundy and was from the twelfth century the capital and residence of the Dukes, until in 1477 the Crown again took possession of the town.
The Carthusian monastery of Champmol (now an asylum) was founded in 1383 by Duke Philip the Bold. It was here that Claus Sluter (of Netherlands extraction, and leading member of the Netherlands-Burgundian school of sculptors) wrought the famous Moses Fountain.

40 DÔLE (Jura). The view from the Place aux Fleurs looking towards the tower of the Church of Nôtre Dame (sixteenth century). Dôle was from the twelfth century onwards the capital of Franche Comté with its own university and parliament (both transferred to Besançon in 1648), until in 1678 it finally went to France under the terms of the Treaty of Nijmegen.

41–42 The river DOUBS above Besançon, on the road to Belfort. Although the distance from its source to the point where it joins the Saône, if taken as the crow flies, is only 60 miles, the Doubs flows for 270 miles, first in a north-easterly then in a south-westerly direction parallel with the line of the Jura, partly through Swiss territory.

43 BOURG-EN-BRESSE (Ain), principal town of the county of Bresse, belonged first to Burgundy, then to Savoy and, since 1601, to France. The church of BROU, on the edge of the town, was built between 1506 and 1532 by Margaret of Austria, daughter of the Emperor Maximilian and Mary of Burgundy (known to us from Goethe's *Egmont* as Stadtholder of the Netherlands), to house the tomb of her second husband, Philip, Count of Bresse and Duke of Savoy (Philibert le Beau)—who died after a short and happy marriage—and those of his mother, Margaret Bourbon, and herself. The excessively ornate marble memorials are the work of Flemish sculptors; the design is by John of Brussels; the figures of the three deceased persons are by Conrad Meidt.
The tomb of Margaret of Austria, which is roofed with a heavy canopy, contains the figure of the princess asleep and below it another of her in death.

44 SALINS-LES-BAINS (Jura), dominated by Fort Belin, lies in a typical Jura landscape in the narrow valley of

the Furieuse. The place owes its importance—formerly much greater than it is now—to salt making, the timber trade, its position as a fortified frontier town, and more recently, as a spa, to its tourist traffic.

45 LYONS, chief city of the Departement Rhône, situated at the confluence of the Rhône and the Saône, the seat of a university (1808) and an archbishop, has been since the fifteenth century the centre of the silk industry introduced from Italy. With some 440,000 inhabitants it is the third largest city in France. *Lugdunum* ("Ravens' Hill"), situated at the crossroads of important trade routes, was developed by Augustus to become the capital of Celtic Gaul. In the Middle Ages Lyons became an imperial city and in 1307 under the leadership of its archbishop it acceded to France.

The Town Hall (Hôtel de Ville) was built between 1646 and 1667 by Simon Maupin and renovated in 1702 by Hardouin-Mansart.

46 MACON, principal town of the Departement Saône-et-Loire, one of the most important places of the Aedui, site of the Roman *Castrum Matisconense*, came under French rule in the thirteenth century during the reign of St. Louis, belonged to Burgundy for a time during the fifteenth, and was a Huguenot stronghold in the sixteenth century. A stone bridge with twelve arches connects this town, so famous for its wines, with St. Laurent (Ain) on the opposite bank of the Saône.

47 PONT-ST-ESPRIT (Gard) owes its name to the bridge which the Bridge-Brothers (Frères Pontifes) built here between 1265 and 1309 under the sign of the Holy Spirit (Saint Esprit). In the Middle Ages it was the only stone bridge over the Rhône between Lyons and Avignon. Our picture shows the town with its churches of St. Saturnin and Saint-Esprit, both dating from the fifteenth century, as seen from the bridge, which is over 1,000 yards long.

48 VIENNE (Isère) on the left bank of the Rhône, the capital of the Allobroges, became the Roman colony *Vienna* in 47 B.C. and in 413 the capital of the first Burgundian empire. It was later the centre of the county of Viennois and in 1448 passed to France. From 450 to 1790 Vienne was the see of an archbishop who bore the title "Primat des primats des Gaules". The former cathedral of St. Maurice rises from a terrace by the Rhône and it acquired its present form between the twelfth and sixteenth centuries. The three west porches dating from the fourteenth and fifteenth centuries serve to show, even in its present damaged state, the richness and fine quality of the original sculptural decoration.

49 GRENOBLE (Isère), with some 100,000 inhabitants, is a university town and centre of a diocese. This most important town in the French Alps grew out of the village of the Allobrogi called Cularo, which the Emperor Gratianus raised to the status of a town and named *Gratianopolis*. It was subsequently the seat of a feudal prince of the Burgundian Empire, who from 1140 onwards called himself Dauphin. When the region became part of France in 1349 this title was transferred to the heir of the French throne and the Dauphiné, which went with the title, became an appanage of his.

Looking across the river towards that part of the town which lies on the right bank one sees the monastery chapel of Sainte-Marie d'en Haut and the fortified hill crowned by the Fort de la Bastille; the fortifications were developed by Vauban, the great military engineer of Louis XIV.

50 On the southern shore of the LAKE OF GENEVA, is EVIAN-LES-BAINS (Haute Savoie), the largest spa and tourist resort on the French side of Lac Léman, with its alkaline mineral springs. The 50-mile-long Lake of Geneva, 1,000 ft. above sea level, with the Rhône flowing through it, is surrounded for the greater part by Swiss territory and is the largest lake in the region of the Alps.

51 ANNECY, the principal town of the Departement Haute-Savoie, was from the tenth to the fifteenth century the seat of the Counts of Genevois, and in 1401 became part of Savoy; along with Savoy it finally went to France as a result of the plebiscite of 1860. As the Reformation triumphed in neighbouring Geneva in 1535, the Bishop and the Cathedral Chapter moved to Annecy.

The Canal du Thiou runs through the ancient part of the town where stands the "Palais de l'Isle", a conglomeration of old buildings.

52 The GRANDE CHARTREUSE (Isère), the original monastery of the Carthusians, lies in the middle of that chalk massif in the lower alps of the Dauphiné, which is called after it. It was here in 1084 that St. Bruno, a native of Cologne and at one time active at Rheims, together with six companions founded the first settlement of the order. The present-day extensive buildings arose mainly in 1676 after the monastery had been burnt down for the eighth time. The monks were banished from 1793 to 1816 and the law of 1901 again denied them residence in France, until they were readmitted under Pétain.

53 The road from Cluses to Chamonix follows the course of the foaming Arve and winds through the gorge which the river has carved as an outlet into the VALLEY OF CHAMONIX. The Aiguille du Gôuter (12,580 feet) is the first of the peaks of the massive Mont Blanc range to come into sight.

54 The view from the Chamonix valley (about 300 feet above sea level) looking towards the granite mass of MONT BLANC (15,780 feet) with its mantle of snow. This, the highest peak in Europe, was first climbed in 1786 by Jacques Balmat; the famous ascent by the Genevese scientist de Saussure was achieved in the following year.

55 The view from the Montanvert near Chamonix, of the MER DE GLACE looking towards the Aiguille du Tacul (11,300 feet), behind which lie the Grandes Jorasses, hidden by clouds. The Mer de Glace is nearly 4 miles long (9 miles including extensions) and in places well over 750 yards wide.

56 BRIANÇON (Hautes-Alpes) lies 3,940 feet above sea level at the junction of the Izoard Pass, the Col du Lautaret and the Montgenèvre Pass leading in the direction of Turin. The fortifications of this strategically important place were restored by Vauban, and even as recently as 1940 Fort Janus, perched high above the town, was instrumental in bringing an Italian attack to a standstill.

The steep, narrow streets of the old part of the town, the "ville haute", with gutters running down the centre between the steps, lead up to the church built between 1702 and 1726.

57 EMBRUN (Hautes-Alpes), the Roman *Ebrodunum*, became under the Emperor Hadrian the chief city of the region of the Alpes Maritimes and in the fourth century the see of a bishop, and subsequently of an archbishop (until 1791). From the terrace of the Promenade du Roc one looks out over the valley of the Durance and across to the Montagne du Grand Morgon.

58 On the road from CORPS to ST. FIRMIN (Hautes-Alpes); this stretch forms part of the "Route Napoléon" opened in 1932. The road follows as far as Grenoble the route taken by Napoleon after his landing in the Golfe-Juan on 1st March, 1815, following his escape from Elba.

59 SISTERON (Basses Alpes), the ancient *Segustero* on Durance, lies at the head of the southern foothills of the Alps at the point of entry into Provence and is dominated by a citadel. This picturesque little town was severely damaged during the fighting in 1944. (This photograph was taken in 1948.)

60 CASTELLANE (Basses-Alpes), above which rises a mass of limestone about 600 feet high called "le Roc". In the foreground is the spacious Place Marcel Sauvaire of this small town situated on the right bank of the river Verdon.

61 Below Castellane the VERDON, a tributary of the Durance, has carved a series of gorges, which have cut deeply into the high limestone plateau of Upper Provence. The GRAND CAÑON DU VERDON is particularly impressive.

62 GRASSE (Alpes-Maritimes), which formed a small city-republic in the Middle Ages, is situated on terraces which fall away towards the south; at the point where the plateau ends begin those abundantly fertile, densely settled slopes and plains which extend down to the Mediterranean. Roses, olives, oranges and other flowers and fruits thrive particularly around Grasse, which is well known for its perfumeries among other things. The former cathedral dating from the twelfth century dominates the old town.

63 The "GRANDE CORNICHE", which Napoleon had built, follows the alignment of a road constructed by

the Romans under Marcus Aurelius. It leads via La Turbie in behind the small principality of Monaco and along those steep slopes of the southernmost foothills of the Alps which plunge into the sea.

64 ANTIBES (Alpes-Maritimes), nowadays a flower-growing centre on the French Riviera, is the *Antipolis* (i.e. "the town opposite", denoting the site of the new settlement facing that of the old village of the earlier inhabitants) which the Greeks of Massilia (Marseilles) founded in the fifth century B.C. as one of their trading posts on the Ligurian coast. Parts of the town walls dating from the sixteenth century and the Château are still preserved. Antibes was fortified for the last time by Vauban as a frontier town facing Savoy.

65 CAP MARTIN (Alpes-Maritimes), a tongue of land jutting out between Monte Carlo and Menton, covered with pine and olive groves and dotted with aristocratic private residences.

66 NICE, or Nizza, chief town of the Departement Alpes-Maritimes with 182,000 inhabitants, is by far the largest place on the French Riviera or Côte d'Azur, and a centre of international tourist traffic. It owes its name *Nicaea* to a victory which the inhabitants of Massilia (Marseilles) gained here over the Ligurians. Throughout its eventful history during the Middle Ages, when it came in turn under the sway of the north Italian cities, the Dukes of Savoy and the Counts of Provence and had to defend itself against pirate raids from seaward, it managed to retain a good measure of civic freedom. It was only through the treaty and plebiscite of 1860 that Nice together with the French Riviera was finally ceded to France by Savoy and Sardinia. The PROMENADE DES ANGLAIS, Nice's fine sea-front along the Baie des Anges, was laid out in 1822–4, the cost being defrayed by the English colony, which was then already considerable.

67 MENTON or Mentone (Alpes-Maritimes), lying at the point where the Italian Riviera begins, is the easternmost of the famous health resorts of the Côte d'Azur, which are patronized particularly during the winter but also at other seasons. Thanks to a sheltered position, the vegetation here is particularly luxuriant and the lemon trees bear blossom and fruit the whole year round. The old part of the town rises in terraces above the harbour of the Baie de Garavan, dominated by the spire of the church of St. Michel.

68 MARSEILLES, chief city of the Departement Bouches-du-Rhône, with some 550,000 inhabitants, is the second largest city of France and its most important commercial port. It was founded as long ago as 600 B.C. by Phocaeans from Asia Minor. *Massalia* (in Greek) or *Massilia* (in Latin) was even in ancient times one of the most important harbours in the Mediterranean, and the rival of Carthage. The entry of Louis XIV in 1660 put a seal on the accession of Provence to the Kingdom of France. Following the conquest of Algeria by France and the opening of the Suez Canal the port gained much in importance.
The entrance to the Old Harbour where, from the time of the Phocaeans right up to the construction of modern quays in the nineteenth and twentieth centuries, all the shipping was handled, is guarded on the left by Fort Saint Jean or Grasse-Tilly, the former castle of the Knights of Malta, and on the right by Fort Saint Nicolas or d'Entrecasteaux, built by Vauban between 1660 and 1665. In January 1943 the Germans razed the old harbour quarter and demolished the Pont Transbordeur which spanned the entrance and had been a prominent feature of the town since 1905.

69 SANARY-SUR-MER (Var) is one of the typical small harbour towns of the Côte d'Azur.

70 The rocky Mediterranean coast with Cap Canaille at CASSIS (Bouches-du-Rhône).

71–77 The island of CORSICA, which constitutes a Departement in itself (Corse), was conquered by the Romans only after a century of effort and was for a long time part of the area under control of Byzantium (Constantinople). In the eleventh century the Pope ceded it to the Pisans and from the thirteenth century onwards it was under Genoese rule. On 15th August, 1769, Napoleon Bonaparte's birthday, the island was annexed by France. Ill. 71 shows a Genoese tower fortress on the Corsican east coast near Bastia.

72 An olive grove at AJACCIO, the capital of Corsica, situated on the Gulf of Ajaccio, with a population of 40,000.

73 The road between Piana and Porto on the west side of Corsica leads through the CALANCHE, steep crags of red granite, which here form the coastline.

74 The COL DE BAVELLA, in southern Corsica between Solenzara and Zonza, is 4,080 feet above sea level. The mountainous interior of the island, which like Sardinia, is a remnant of the former continental Tyrrhenis, rises to a height of 8,890 feet (Monte Cinto).

75 The town of BONIFACIO lies at the southern tip of Corsica on the plateau of a peninsula, the white chalk cliffs of which here drop 200 feet into the sea. Slightly less than eight miles to the south, across the Straits of Bonifacio, lies the coast of Sardinia.
Bonifacio was founded in 828 by the Marquis Bonifacio of Tuscany and in the Middle Ages it was strongly fortified as protection against raids by pirates.

76 In ERBALUNGA, a hamlet near Bastia in Corsica.

77 BASTIA, whose population now numbers 53,000, is the largest town and most important centre of commerce in Corsica. It was founded in 1380 by the Genoese. Its oldest part is the "Terra Vecchia" around the old harbour; with its tall and crowded houses and the church of Saint Jean-Baptiste it presents the picture of a typical Mediterranean coastal town.

78–79 LES BAUX (Bouches-du-Rhône), quite unique of its kind, stands on an isolated rock mass of the Alpilles, whose bare chalk cliffs rise above the olive groves of mid-Provence. The place gave its name to bauxite which was discovered here in 1822 and acquired special importance as the new material for the production of aluminium. The warlike lords of Baux became extraordinarily powerful in the Middle Ages; they called themselves Prince of Orange, King of Arles and even Emperor of Constantinople at various times, and in the thirteenth century the song of the troubadours and the cult of courtly love flourished here. Under the Manville family, who lived here as barons under the French Crown, Les Baux became a Protestant stronghold. In 1632 Louis XIII had the castle destroyed, and the town fell into decay; over fifty persons still live among its ruins.

80 ORANGE (Vaucluse) was once *Arausio*, a Roman town of some importance on the great Rhône highway. The triumphal arch, which stands in the middle of the modern Route Nationale, is by reason of its size and the richness of its decoration one of the most notable Roman monuments of its kind. Its reliefs recall the deeds of Caesar's Second Legion, the veterans of which formed the colony of Arausio. In the eleventh century Orange became an independent county, and in the twelfth a principality, which later passed to the House of Nassau (1530) and so gave its name to the Dutch dynasty. In 1622 Moritz of Nassau used the stones of the Roman buildings, which had already been pillaged by the Alemanni and the Visigoths, to build a mighty castle, which Louis XIV then had razed to the ground. Of the flourishing Roman town of old only the amphitheatre and this triumphal arch remain.

81 ST. RÉMY-DE-PROVENCE (Bouches-du-Rhône). Outside the small town of today, at the foot of the Alpilles, there stand on the "Plateau des Antiques" the so-called Mausoleum and the triumphal arch of the Roman *Glanum*, near which the foundations of a Greco-Gallic town of the second or third century B.C. have recently been excavated. The triumphal arch was presumably built immediately before or after Caesar's death and is the oldest Roman triumphal arch in existence. The other monument is a cenotaph, a memorial to someone who died in the early days of the Empire; it is in an exceptionally fine state of preservation.

82, 84 ARLES (Bouches-du-Rhône) owes its place in history above all to its bridge, the southernmost crossing of the Rhône on the route from Italy to Spain. Notable buildings and monuments dating from a wide range of periods have here been preserved. The rise of the Roman *Arelate* (Celtic "marshy place") began when Caesar developed a military colony here.
The Roman amphitheatre was built in the time of Augustus and seated about 7,000 spectators. Since for centuries it served later generations as a quarry, only parts of it could be restored. The stage wall was about three times as high as the two columns shown in the picture.

83 NÎMES, the chief town of the Departement Gard and today an industrial and commercial centre with over

100,000 inhabitants, a large proportion of whom are Protestants, grew up around a sacred spring. The Gauls of *Nemausus* subjected themselves to Roman rule as early as 121 B.C. Augustus settled his veterans here and thereafter the town enjoyed the special favour of the Roman Emperors, particularly under Antoninus Pius who was himself a native of Nîmes. The ARENA of the time of Augustus is so well preserved, despite the fact that the Visigoths turned it into a fortress in the fifth century, that it can even now be used, like that of Arles, for public spectacles, in particular the Provençal bull fights. It was originally capable of accommodating 21,000 spectators.

84 LES ALISCAMPS, i.e. the *Elyssii Campi* or Elysian Fields of ARLES (see also Ill. 82) were from classical times to the Middle Ages one of the most famous of cemeteries and were even extolled in the verse of Dante and Ariosto. The tombs were later used as building stone and the finest sarcophagi were removed. Several of these sarcophagi are preserved in the Museum of Christian Art at Arles.

85 The PONT DU GARD, one of the most impressive monuments of Roman civil engineering, spans the Gard at the foot of the Cevennes; it is 885 feet long and 160 feet high, with three tiers of 6, 11 and 35 arches respectively. The aqueduct formed part of the water supply system which was built by Agrippa, Augustus' son-in-law, and delivered water from the region of Uzès to Nîmes about 30 miles away with an average fall of about 21 inches to the mile.

86 AIX-EN-PROVENCE (Bouches-du-Rhône). The Cours Mirabeau, an avenue of plane trees planted in the seventeenth century to replace the town wall, with the Fontaine des Neuf-Canons. *Aquae Sextiae* owes its name to the Consul Sextius Calvinus (123 B.C.) and was esteemed by the Romans on account of its warm springs. Aix became in the thirteenth century the residence of the Counts of Provence. Following its incorporation into France in 1481 it was regarded as the capital city of Provence, and a Parliament functioned here between 1501 and 1790. It is the seat of an archbishop and a university founded in 1413.

87 MONTMAJOUR ABBEY (Bouches-du-Rhône) was founded in the sixth century by St. Cézaire, Bishop of Arles; it was endowed by Charlemagne and acquired its Romanesque church in the twelfth century. The fortified tower close by the church was added in the fourteenth century. In the Middle Ages it was the goal of great numbers of pilgrims. After a period of decay magnificent new buildings were erected, but Louis XVI caused the monastery to be dissolved in 1786 when the last abbot, Cardinal Rohan, was compromised by the affair of the Queen's necklace. The Abbey was sold to a woman dealer who in turn sold the contents and had part of the new buildings demolished and carted away. (In the background on the right of the picture can be seen a wing of the eighteenth century buildings, several storeys high, which has been left standing.)

88 TARASCON (Bouches-du-Rhône), the home of Tartarin, the delightful character of Alphonse Daudet's novels, stands on the left bank of the Rhône. The town owes its name to a monster, the "Tarasque" which was overcome by St. Martha. The castle was built in the twelfth century on the site of a castrum of the Roman legionaries, and was extended in the fifteenth century by "Good King René", Count of Provence, who resided alternately here and at Aix.

89–91 AVIGNON, chief town of the Departement Vaucluse, the Roman *Avenio*, in the Middle Ages an independent city-republic, reached its zenith in the fourteenth century when the Popes had their residence here (1309–76) during the "Babylonian captivity" of the Church. John XXII, who became Pope in 1316 and who was himself a native of Avignon, enlarged the existing bishop's palace, and his successors further extended it so that it became one of the greatest Gothic secular buildings, to outward appearance a grim fortress but with an interior furnished with all the magnificence of a rich princely court.

Ill. 89 presents the view from the island in the Rhône looking towards the Palace of the Popes and the church of Notre Dame-des-Domes rising above the city wall and the houses; on the left is the hill of the Rocher des Doms laid out with gardens. In Ill. 90 the palace is seen from the church of St. Pierre, that is, from the southern side. Ill. 91 shows the southern part of the west front built by Clement VI (1342–52), with the windows of the great audience chamber below, and those of the papal chapel on the floor above.

92 MARTIGUES (Bouches-du-Rhône) is a fishing port on the Etang de Berre, a lagoon in the region of the Rhône estuary. Corot and countless other artists have recorded the picturesque aspects of this "Provençal Venice".

93–94 AIGUES-MORTES (Gard), situated in the midst of salt marshes and now three miles inland, was founded in the thirteenth century by Saint Louis as the point of departure for his crusade. His son, Philip the Bold, built the town walls, which are still perfectly preserved; they form an irregular quadrilateral, 620 and 544 yards long, 329 and 294 yards broad, and contain fifteen towers and ten gates.

95 SAINT-GILLES (Gard) possesses in the façade of its abbey church a leading example of Romanesque art in southern France, a work rivalling in importance the porch of St. Trophine at Arles. The abbey was founded in the seventh or eighth century by St. Aegidius (St. Gilles), who came from Greece. The porches built between 1180 and 1240 show the direct influence of classical architecture; their rich sculptural ornamentation is the product of various workshops.

96 AGDE (Hérault) on the bank of the River Hérault just above its estuary, has largely lost its importance, as a port, to the neighbouring Sète. From about 400 until 1790 it was the centre of a diocese. In the twelfth century the former cathedral of Saint-Etienne was turned into a fortress built of the dark volcanic basalt of the district; this conversion was carried out because of the many attacks upon the town in the Middle Ages.

97 ELNE (Pyrénées-Orientales), the Roman *Illiberis*, was given its name Helena (*Castrum Helenae*) in memory of the mother of the Emperor Constantine. The bishopric which was founded in 571 was transferred to Perpignan in 1602. The Romanesque cloisters belong to the former cathedral of Sainte-Eulalie dating from the eleventh and twelfth centuries; the magnificent capitals illustrate scenes from the Old and New Testaments.

98 BÉZIERS (Hérault), a town of 60,000 inhabitants lying among the vineyards of Languedoc, was in Roman times the station of the Seventh Legion (*Baeterrae Septimanorum*). In 1209 this Albigensian stronghold was destroyed by Simon de Montfort. The old town with its former, fortress-like cathedral of Saint-Nazaire (twelfth to fourteenth centuries) stands on the right bank of the Orb, which is here crossed by the Pont Vieux, a thirteenth-century bridge with seventeen arches.

99 PERPIGNAN, principal town of the Departement Pyrenées-Orientales with 65,000 inhabitants, the old seat of the house of Roussillon, belonged from 1172 to Aragon. Its most brilliant period was from 1276–1462 when it was the capital of the small kingdom of Mallorca. It finally acceded to France in 1660. The great trees of the Promenade des Platanes were planted in 1809.

100–1 The ROUTE DE CORNICHE runs from Collioure to the Spanish frontier via BANYULS (Pyrénées-Orientales) and follows the southernmost part of the French Mediterranean coast. Some of the Monts Albères, the eastern foothills of the Pyrenees, drop steeply to the sea and form the bays and coves in which the fishing ports lie. Some of the vineyards slope down to the coast. Banyuls, thanks to its unusually equable climate, is well adapted both as a winter and a summer resort and is famous for its wine.

102 COLLIOURE (Pyrénées-Orientales), as a fishing port with its brilliant colourings, is the ideal place for painters and other guests. Its fortifications testify to its importance, since ancient times, as the gateway leading from the plain of Perpignan to the Mediterranean. In the fifteenth century representatives from Genoa, Venice and Florence were resident here. The old château by the harbour, a castle of the Templars dating from the twelfth century, was renovated by Vauban.

103 FOIX, chief town of the Departement Ariège, is dominated by the castle hill with its towers dating from the twelfth, fourteenth and fifteenth centuries, the seat of the powerful Counts of Foix. The place grew up around an oratory established by Charlemagne, which in the tenth century developed into the Abbey of St. Volusien.

104 Above the village of Gavarnie (Hautes-Pyrénées) situated at over 4,400 feet, the peaks of the Pyrenees,

rising to close on 10,000 feet, constitute the frontier between France and Spain; with their glaciers and waterfalls they form the head of the valley, and are known as the CIRQUE DE GAVARNIE.

105 MUSCULDY, a village in the Basque country of the Basses-Pyrénées.

106 MONTRÉJEAU (Haute-Garonne) grew out of a hamlet called Montreal-de-Rivière on the Garonne. The Town Hall is accommodated in the upper floor of the covered Market (Les Halles).

107 BAYONNE (Basses-Pyrénées), the largest town in that part of the French Pyrenees which is inhabited by the Basques, was originally called *Lapurdum* and gave the region its name of Labourd; the name *Baiona* only gained currency in the twelfth century. Bayonne belonged to Aquitaine and so remained in English possession for three centuries; in 1451 it defended itself against French occupation.
The Cathedral of Sainte-Marie, one of the most important of the southern French Gothic churches, was begun in 1213 and continued in the fourteenth and fifteenth centuries. The fine cloisters date from the thirteenth century.

108 A canal near CÉRONS (Gironde) in the Bordeaux region. The canals with their avenues of trees form just as much a part of the French landscape, from north to south, as do the shaded Routes Nationales.

109–10 The CITÉ OF CARCASSONNE, with its double ring of walls and battlements, with its castle and towers and pinnacles, offers an example, in an unparalleled state of preservation, of a great mediaeval fortress. The early mediaeval town was built in Languedoc at the foot of the Pyrenees on Roman-Visigothic foundations. St. Louis took possession of it during the Albigensian wars and resettled the inhabitants in the lower town of the fruitful plain (1247). Here the modern Carcassonne developed into the principal city of the Departement Aude, and now has a population of 32,000. Since that resettlement the Cité or upper town has remained almost intact as nothing more than a fortress on its hill.

111 One of the scattered farms in the fertile, rolling Albigeois countryside, to the east of Albi.

112 ALBI, chief town of the Departement Tarn, stands on the left bank of the river Tarn. The old capital of the Albigenses became the seat of a bishop as early as the third century; in the twelfth and thirteenth centuries it was one of the centres of the Albigensian heresy which spread over the entire south of France and was suppressed with much bloodshed. The cathedral of Sainte-Cécile built between 1282 and 1390 is an imposing brick structure with a fortress-like tower (the upper part of which dates from the fifteenth century). Below, spanning the Tarn, is one of the oldest bridges in France, the Pont Vieux, built in 1035.

113 MONTAUBAN, chief town of the Departement Tarn-et-Garonne, and since 1317 a bishop's see was one of the chief strongholds of the Huguenots in the sixteenth and seventeenth centuries until Richelieu had its fortifications razed. The brick bridge over the Tarn dates from 1303–16. In the background is the church of Saint-Jacques, a brick construction of the fourteenth and fifteenth centuries, with an octagonal tower.

114 CAHORS, principal town of the Departement Lot, was once *Cadurcum*, the chief centre of the Gallic tribe of the Cadurci. The Romans called it *Divona* after a sacred spring; in the Middle Ages it was the capital of Quercy. The PONT VALENTRÉ, begun in 1308, is one of the best preserved of Gothic fortified bridges, with six arches and three tower gates.

115 TOULOUSE, chief city of the Departement Haute-Garonne, the seat of an archbishop and a university, has 264,000 inhabitants and is one of the most important cultural centres in the French provinces, with an artistic and scientific tradition going back to the Romans. In the fifth century *Tolosa* was capital of the kingdom of the Visigoths; in the Middle Ages the Counts of Toulouse were among the most powerful of the lords of the south of France. In 1271 Toulouse came under the French Crown and became the capital of Languedoc with its own parliament.
The sixteenth century, despite the religious conflicts, was a period of intense building activity in which the sculptor and architect Nicolas Bachelier, a native of the town, played a prominent part. He designed among other things the HOTEL D'ASSÉZAT with its

characteristic Renaissance courtyard, one of the most beautiful of the rich private houses of the period. Its last owner bequeathed it in 1895 to the learned societies of Toulouse, the most famous of which is the Académie des Jeux Floraux.

116 In the Middle Ages MOISSAC (Tarn-et-Garonne) possessed a powerful Benedictine Abbey which was one of the first to accept the Cluny reforms. Two of the most outstanding examples of twelfth-century Romanesque art have been preserved from the monastery of Saint-Pierre: the porch of the abbey church and the cloisters. According to an inscription the latter were begun by Abbot Ansquitil in 1100, but only in the thirteenth century did they acquire their pointed arches with the slender marble columns.

117 SOUILLAC (Lot). This relief, representing the Prophet Isaiah, in the west porch of the Romanesque church, which formerly belonged to an abbey, in one of the greatest achievements of the so-called Aquitainian sculpture of the twelfth century.

118 BORDEAUX, the chief city of the Gironde with 254,000 inhabitants. As *Burdigala*, it was a flourishing centre of commerce even in Roman times, and from the fourth century it was the principal town of Aquitania Secunda. For three hundred years Bordeaux was under the English crown, until in 1453 it declared its allegiance to Charles VII of France. Trade in the famous Bordeaux wines plays the greatest part in its economy. The PLACE DES QUICONCES is the centre of extensive grounds, most of which were laid out in the eighteenth century. Two rostral columns, which serve as lighthouses, stand on the bank of the Garonne which here forms a large harbour basin.

119 SAINT-EMILION (Gironde), whose red wines have a special reputation, is dominated by the so-called "Clocher isolé", a Romanesque church tower, with a spire dating from the fifteenth century.

120 VINEYARDS NEAR BORDEAUX. About a fifth of the Gironde region is covered by vineyards where the Bordeaux wines are grown. The most notable of the individual wine districts is Médoc, whence come the famous château vintages of Margaux, Lafite, Latour, etc.; the district around Sauternes produces very fine white wines, Château Yquem for example.

121 VILLEFRANCHE-DE-ROUERGUE (Aveyron) was founded in the thirteenth century and had special privileges conferred upon it by the Count of Toulouse, which is how it came to be designated "Ville franche". A fine fountain decorates the Place Notre-Dame, the centre of the small, old-world town.

122 CONQUES (Aveyron), a remote little place standing on a tributary of the Lot, owes its fame to the Romanesque church of Sainte-Foy, which belonged to one of the richest French abbeys of the Middle Ages. This church was built between 1035 and 1060; it possesses some exceptionally fine sculpture and a remarkable collection of church treasures dating from the ninth to the sixteenth centuries.

123-4 THE TARN GORGES (Gorges du Tarn) cut their way through the Causses (Causse de Sauveterre and Causse Méjean) for some 30 miles between Florac and Millau; the River Tarn has here carved into the flat uplands of the south-western Cevennes to a depth of about 600 to 1,200 feet and in the gorges thus formed has laid bare the almost horizontal chalk strata.
The first of our illustrations shows the little town of SAINTE-ÉNIMIE (Lozère), so called after a Merovingian princess who was cured here at the Burle spring and founded a convent. It lies deep in the valley at a bend in the Tarn. The picture on the right depicts "les Détroits", where the valley becomes a narrow ravine.

125-6 MILLAU (Aveyron), a town of 15,000 inhabitants, lies where the Tarn leaves the Causses for the fertile plain and joins the Dourbie. The Romans had firmly established themselves here in 122 B.C., and the pottery of *Castrum Aemilianum* was known far and wide. In the sixteenth century Millau joined the Reformation and in 1629 suffered particularly, following the revocation of the Edict of Nantes. Only in the nineteenth century did the well-known and very old-established manufacture of gloves (of lambskin) flourish once more. The PLACE DE L'HÔTEL DE VILLE (Ill. 126), with its houses of the twelfth to the sixteenth centuries and its "Empire" fountain, presents a particularly charming example of the sleepy old southern French provincial town.

127 LES EYZIES-DE-TAYAC (Dordogne), where the Beune flows into the Vézère, is a centre of archaeological

research, with a National Museum of Archaeology. Under the rock walls of the Vézère valley in the immediate vicinity of Les Eyzies and in the surrounding neighbourhood, caves have been discovered since 1863 containing evidence of human habitation—parts of skeletons, tools, *graffiti* and paintings on the rock; these discoveries have thrown new light on the subject of prehistoric races and their cultural development.

128–9 LA ROCHELLE, chief town of the Departement Charente-Maritime with some 50,000 inhabitants, was at its peak from the fourteenth to the seventeenth centuries. It was a stronghold of the Huguenots; in 1571 the reformed churches of France united here on the "Symbole de la Rochelle". In 1628 the town, which had allied itself with England, had to surrender to Richelieu's troops after fifteen months of siege, and lost the religious freedom which had earlier been granted to it. La Rochelle was the principal port for traffic with Canada and other French overseas possessions.

Around the OLD HARBOUR (Vieux Port), which is still used by the larger fishing boats, the town has preserved an old-world aspect of particular charm and colourfulness. The entrance to the harbour (Ill. 128) is guarded by the two mighty towers de la Chaine and Saint-Nicolas which date from the fourteenth century. On the town side (Ill. 129) the scene is dominated by the Great Clock Gate Tower (Porte de la Grosse-Horloge), built in the thirteenth and seventeenth centuries.

130 PÉRIGUEUX, chief town of the Departement Dordogne with about 40,000 inhabitants, grew on the right bank of the River Isle from a union of the Cité, the ancient *Vesuna*, centre of the Petrocorii, with the high-lying Bourg du Puy-Saint-Front, which were once rivals. The church of Saint-Front, built over the tomb of Saint-Front, the Apostle of Périgord, dominates the town as seen from the river. It originally belonged to the Abbey and only in 1669 did it become the cathedral in place of Saint-Etienne. This peculiar Romanesque building, showing strong Byzantine influence, dates presumably from the first half of the twelfth century. In the nineteenth century it was heavily restored and it was then that the belfry was added.

131 COGNAC (Charente), birthplace of King Francis I, owes its world-wide reputation to the brandy made here, which is produced from the vines of the Champagne de Cognac (Grande or Fine Champagne and Petite Champagne) and the surrounding districts. The Pont Neuf links the town on the left bank of the Charente with the Faubourg St. Jacques.

132 ANGOULÊME, chief town of the Departement Charente with about 40,000 inhabitants, has been a bishop's see since the third century. The Cathedral of Saint-Pierre, which dates mainly from the first half of the twelfth century and was largely restored in the nineteenth, possesses a magnificent Romanesque façade containing seventy-five figures which represent the Day of Judgment.

133 LA CHAISE-DIEU (Haute-Loire) is the seat of a Benedictine abbey which was founded in 1044 by St. Robert. The attached church of SAINT-ROBERT, one of the major achievements of Gothic architecture in the Auvergne, was rebuilt between 1343 and 1352 by Pope Clement VI (Pierre-Roger de Beaufort), a former monk of the monastery, and completed between 1370 and 1378 by his nephew, Pope Gregory XI. A stone rood-loft separates the nave from the choir which is on the same level and contains the tomb of Clement XI.

134 The volcanic plateau of MURAT in the Cantal with the little town of the same name lying at an altitude of nearly 3,000 feet on the River Alagnon between basalt peaks.

135–6 LE PUY, chief town of the Departement Haute-Loire with about 20,000 inhabitants, lies in a sort of amphitheatre on Mont Anis, one of the volcanic hills of "Puys" (from the Latin *podium*) which are characteristic of the Auvergne. At the highest point, on the Rocher Corneille, there has stood since 1860 the colossal statue of Notre-Dame-de-France, which was made from the guns captured at Sebastopol. The old principal centre of Velay, the region of the Vellavi, received in the Middle Ages the designation "Podium Sanctae Mariae" and with its shrine of Notre-Dame was one of the most famous places of pilgrimage in France, visited already by Charlemagne among others. In the suburb of Aiguille stands the ROCHER

D'AIGUILLE (Ill. 135), a volcanic rocky prominence, on which the church of Saint Michel d'Aiguille was built in the tenth century.

137 The LAC DE GUÉRY, nearly 4,000 feet above sea level, is one of the lakes in the chain of the Monts-Dore and the Puys, where the Auvergne and France's central mountain-range reach their highest point (Puy de Sancy, 6,190 feet). The water is held back by the lava mass.

138 LE MONT-DORE (Puy-de-Dome), one of the best known spas in France, lies at 3,450 feet in the middle of the Mont-Dore massif on the banks of the Dordogne. The radio-active medicinal springs, which flow from the volcanic rock at temperatures up to 116°F., were already known in ancient times. The Roman baths were even greater in extent than the modern establishments built towards the end of the nineteenth century.

139–40 Following the road leading from Le Mont-Dore through the mountains of the Auvergne to Clermont-Ferrand and passing the Lac de Guéry (Ill. 137), you come to the rocky mass of the ROCHER SANADOIRE (Ill. 139), 4,225 feet high, beyond which extend the lowland and the vale of Rochefort. Later you come in sight of the rounded peaks of the MONTS DÔMES in the region of Clermont (Ill. 140).

141 MOULINS, chief town of the Departement Allier, was the residence of the Dukes of Bourbon from the fourteenth century onwards. The church of Notre-Dame, a cathedral church since 1822, possesses in its choir (1465–1507) an outstanding example of late French Gothic in the *flamboyant* style. In the vestry there is the triptych of the Master of Moulins, one of the major works of fifteenth-century painting.

142 BOURGES, the principal town of the Departement Cher with over 40,000 inhabitants, the ancient *Avaricum*, was captured by Caesar in 52 B.C. and has been a bishop's see since the third century. Bourges was the residence of King Charles VII in the fifteenth century.

The Cathedral of Saint Stephen (Saint-Etienne), begun in 1192 and consecrated in 1324, is one of the most magnificent achievements of French Gothic architecture. The rich façade with its five porches matches the spacious nave with its double aisles on either side. On the tympanum of the centre porch there is a representation of the Last Judgment.

143 SAINT-BENOIT-SUR-LOIRE (Loiret) was the seat of an abbey which owed its fame and wealth to its relics of St. Benedict. In the seventh century the Abbot of Fleury had the Saint's remains brought from the destroyed Monte Cassino and thereafter Fleury became St. Benoit. The abbey church was built between 1087 and 1218; its western fore-structure, open on the ground floor and with richly sculptured capitals, is one of the most remarkable examples of Romanesque architecture in France.

144 SULLY-SUR-LOIRE (Loiret). The castle, standing by an important bridge over the Loire, was built as a fortress in the thirteenth and fourteenth centuries. In the fifteenth century it belonged to Georges de la Trémoille and was at times the residence of the Charles VII, who was twice visited here by Joan of Arc. In 1602 the estate was bought by Maximilien de Béthune; this minister, given the title of Duke of Sully by Henry IV, and one of the greatest and most versatile of French statesmen, furnished it magnificently and frequently stayed here. In the eighteenth century Voltaire, who was a friend of the duke of that day, was a frequent guest at Sully. Our photograph was taken before 1940 when the German bombing of the bridge at Sully did considerable damage.

145 NEVERS, chief town of the Departement Nièvre, is an important bridgehead on the right bank of the Loire where it is joined by the Nièvre; as such it suffered from the bombing of 1940, during which part of the cathedral was destroyed. The County of Nevers (Nivernais), which was at times united with Burgundy, was raised to a Duchy by Francis I in 1539. The DUCAL PALACE (Palais ducal), now a court of justice, is a fine Renaissance building, begun in 1475 and finished in the sixteenth century.

146 ORLÉANS, principal city of the Departement Loiret with 65,000 inhabitants, the Celtic *Genabum*, rebelled against the Romans in 52 B.C. and was destroyed by Caesar; in the fourth century it was named *Aurelianum*. In 451 Attila appeared at the gates of the town

but the inhabitants, inspired by their bishop St. Aignan, forced him to withdraw. During the Hundred Years' War, in 1428, Orleans was besieged by the English and relieved on the 8th May by Joan of Arc, the "Maid of Orleans".

In June 1940, people fleeing from the Paris region swarmed across the great bridge over the Loire, trying to reach the South ahead of the German advance. The German bombs not only damaged the George V Bridge, which was built between 1751 and 1761 by Hupeau and Peyronnet, but left the old town of Orleans in ruins. In May 1944 this strategically important place suffered fresh war damage. Our photograph shows the reconstructed George V Bridge.

The thirteenth-century cathedral of Sainte-Croix was partly destroyed in 1567 by the Calvinists and re-erected in the seventeenth and eighteenth centuries in what was at that time taken to be the Gothic style; the two towers—damaged during the second World War—date from that time.

147 GIEN (Loiret), like Orleans a bridgehead on the Loire, which flows across central France from East to West, suffered similarly in the last war by virtue of its strategic importance. Here too the French troops and the fleeing civil population streaming southwards on 15th to 17th June, 1940, caused great congestion while German bombs rained down and destroyed or damaged the castle and the picturesque little old town. The stone bridge with its twelve arches (on the right of the picture) has since been restored and the line of gabled houses across the river has beeen rebuilt. The bridge, castle and other buildings owed their origin or altered design to Anne de Beaujeu, a daughter of Louis XI, who as the Countess of Gien lived here around 1500. To the right of the mediaeval fortress tower stands the castle begun in 1494 and built of white and red bricks with stone door and window frames.

1 8 BLOIS, chief town of the Departement Loir-et-Cher, was the seat of a powerful line of counts from the ninth century onwards until in 1391 it passed by purchase into the possession of the house of Orleans. Of the famous châteaux of the Loire that of Blois is the one most closely linked with French history: it was here that Louis XII was born in 1462, the son of the 71-year-old poet of the house of Orleans, Charles. He and his son-in-law Francis I, made Blois a royal residence. It was Henry III who in this palace used the occasion of the second summoning of the states-general to Blois on 23rd December, 1588, to murder the all-powerful Henry Duke of Guise. In 1617 Louis XIII banished his mother Marie de' Medici to Blois. The magnificence of the buildings matches the historical importance of the palace. Between two remaining parts of the thirteenth-century castle stand the gallery of Charles d'Orléans, the wing built by Louis XII, the wing of Francis I, and the north-west building erected by Mansart for Gaston of Orleans. The contribution of that lover of the arts, Francis I, provides the highlight: forming part of the façade facing the courtyard, which is decorated with the royal emblems—the porcupine of Louis XII and the salamander of Francis I,—rises the tower-like spiral staircase, a masterpiece of the French Renaissance.

149 The Palace of AMBOISE (Indre-et-Loire) stands on a hill on the left bank of the Loire which was fortified from Gallo-Roman times onwards. Here it was that Clovis and Alaric the Visigoth celebrated their short-lived pact. Charles VII confiscated the castle of the Counts of Amboise, Louis XI made it the Queen's residence, and the future Charles VIII was born here. In 1491 the latter began work on the palace, which Louis XII and Francis I completed and which was largely demolished in the nineteenth century. Francis I spent the early part of his reign in Amboise and organized sumptuous entertainments; as a great patron of the arts he invited Leonardo da Vinci to stay at the palace. Leonardo spent the last years of his life here and lies buried in Amboise. The palace later served as a state prison, for Abd-el-Kader among others, and still belongs to the former royal family. From the other bank of the Loire can be seen the Logis du Roi and the broad Tour des Minimes, from which a bridle-path leads down to the Loire.

150 The Palace of CHAMBORD (Loir-et-Cher), the largest of the châteaux of the Loire, was built from 1519 onwards by Francis I on the site of a hunting lodge of the Counts of Blois in the middle of the Forest of Boulogne. It is built in the form of a parallelogram with four round towers at the corners around a square central block; measuring 813 feet by 354 feet, it contains 440 rooms. The reputed architects are Pierre

Neveu, called Trinqueau, and the Italian Dominico de Cortone, who had at their disposal the services of 1,800 workmen for fifteen years. The Emperor Charles V was delighted with the magnificence of his reception when Francis I showed him the palace, then barely finished. The king spent the greater part of the last years of his life in Chambord. His successor, Henry II, completed the building. Louis XIV frequently stayed at Chambord and Molière's *Bourgeois Gentilhomme* was produced here for the first time.

151 The Palace of CHAUMONT (Loir-et-Cher) on the left bank of the Loire was erected by Pierre d'Amboise and his son Charles between 1465 and 1510 in the transitional style between the Gothic and the Renaissance. Catherine de' Medici, Henry II's widow, bought it in 1650 to accommodate her rival Diana of Poitiers. The palace later served as the temporary residence of Madame de Staël when she had been banished from Paris by Napoleon. It is now state property.

152 The Palace of CHEVERNY (Loir-et-Cher) is the perfect example of an aristocratic seat in the classical style of the seventeenth century, with magnificent interior decoration. The building was finished in 1634 according to the directions of Count Hurault de Cheverny and is still in the possession of a descendant of his, the Comte de Vibraye.

153 The Palace of CHENONCEAU (Indre-et-Loire) is the work of Thomas Bohier, *Receveur des Finances* of the realm and of his wife. They did not demolish the fortified tower of the former seat of the de Marques family but extended the palace building from 1513 onwards. The Grande Galerie by the architect Philibert Delorme, forms a bridge over the river Cher. The palace came into the possession of Francis I; Henry II gave it to his mistress, Diana of Poitiers, who in turn had to hand it over to Catherine de' Medici after the death of the king. A nineteenth-century owner had it carefully restored.

154 TOURS, capital of the former province of Touraine and now chief town of the Departement Cher-et-Loire with nearly 80,000 inhabitants, lies between the Loire and the Cher and is the town of St. Martin, the patron saint of France, who as the third bishop of Tours towards the end of the fourth century spread the gospel through the country; his grave became a shrine of pilgrimage. In the sixth century Gregory of Tours, as bishop and historian added to the city's fame, as did also around the year 800 the great scholar Alcuin, who was appointed Abbot of St. Martin by Charlemagne. Louis XI introduced the silk industry into Tours and in the sixteenth century the thriving industrial and commercial town already had at least as many inhabitants as it has today. In October-November 1870, and again in June 1940, the German invasion caused the French Government to move first to Tours, then to Bordeaux. In the fighting of 1940 the old part of the town between the (modern) church of St. Martin and the cathedral was for the most part destroyed.

The cathedral of SAINT-GATIEN, so called after the first bishop of Tours and built between the thirteenth and sixteenth centuries, possesses in its west façade a brilliant example of the late Gothic *flamboyant* style which is in this instance already merging into that of the Renaissance.

155 POITIERS, the principal town of the Departement Vienne with over 40,000 inhabitants, was as *Limonum* the tribal capital of the Celtic Pictavi and received its first bishop in the fourth century in the person of St. Hilarius. In 732 Charles Martell defeated the Arabs at Poitiers (the Battle of Tours and Poitiers) and so saved Christian Europe from the Mohammedan invasion. Charles VII moved the Paris parliament to Poitiers for the period 1423–36 and in 1432 founded a university here.

The Romanesque church of NOTRE-DAME-LA-GRANDE has a fine twelfth-century façade with Old and New Testament scenes in decorative style; in the niches of the upper storeys are statues of the Twelve Apostles, and also Saint Hilarius and Saint Martin.

156 CHINON (Indre-et-Loire), a little old town on the Vienne which is dominated by an elongated castle, is the birthplace of Rabelais. The place, which was fortified even in Roman times, was strengthened by the English Kings Henry II and Richard I (Cœur de Lion) as one of their main bases on the Continent, but it was captured for France by Philip Augustus in 1205.

In the Rue Voltaire is the stone house (on the extreme

left of our picture) to which Richard Cœur de Lion was brought after being wounded at the siege of Châlus and where he died on 6th April, 1109. Next to it stands the Grand Carroi inn where the eighteen-year-old Joan of Arc dismounted in 1429 and spent two whole days in fasting and prayer. When she was finally admitted to the royal court which was then being held at the castle, she did not allow herself to be confused by any of the tests to which she was subjected and at once recognized Charles VI who was hidden among the crowd; from Chinon she went forth as "one sent by God" and began her campaign against the English.

157 The ABBEY OF FONTEVRAULT (Maine-et-Loire) was founded in 1098 by the famous preacher Robert d'Arbrissel, with separate sections for men, women, girls doing penance, lepers and people suffering from other diseases, the whole being placed under the direction of an abbess. The Romanesque church with four squat domes over the nave, and a choir with ample window lighting and unusually tall columns, was built in the twelfth century and was designated by the Plantagenets Henry II and Richard Cœur de Lion as their burial place. Henry's queen, Eleanor of Aquitaine, who spent her last years in the abbey, was buried next to them.

158–9 SAINT-SAVIN-SUR-GARTEMPE (Vienne). In 811 Charlemagne founded an abbey above the tomb of the hermit St. Savin. The abbey church was built in the eleventh century and is preserved intact in its original state with notable paintings of the eleventh and thirteenth centuries on the vaulted ceiling of the central nave and on the walls. Beside the modern bridge there is a Gothic stone bridge of the thirteenth century spanning the River Gartempe.

160 On the bank of the river INDRE near Reignac (Indre-et-Loire).

161 The former CHARTREUSE DU LIGET (Indre-et-Loire) comprises the remains of the Carthusian monastery founded by the English King Henry II.

162 ANGERS, the chief town of the Departement Maine-et Loire and of the former county of Anjou with 86,000 inhabitants, lies on the Maine some few miles above its confluence with the Loire. Various buildings of the important mediaeval town, including the cathedral and the castle, have been preserved. Angers has had a university since 1246. Saint Louis transferred Anjou, as a duchy, to his brother Charles. The last duke was that learned lover of the arts, René ("le bon roi René"), King of the Two Sicilies and Count of Provence, who in the end had to give up Angers to Louis XI and withdraw to Aix. From the right bank of the Maine you obtain a good view of the castle and some of its seventeen bastion-like towers, beyond the Pont de la Basse Chaîne; it was rebuilt by Saint Louis between 1228 and 1238 and partly demolished again by Henry III.

163 NANTES, the principal city of the Departement Loire-Inférieure with some 200,000 inhabitants, lies on the Loire about 30 miles from the sea, and with its outer harbour of Saint-Nazaire is one of the foremost mercantile centres of France; it is also of considerable industrial importance. The tribe of the Namnètes had their main centre here, called *Condivicnum*, which the Romans turned into an administrative and trading centre. Nantes later became the residence of the dukes of Brittany. It was here that Henry IV on 13th August, 1598, proclaimed the Edict of Nantes, which granted the French Protestants certain rights, but which was revoked by Louis XIV in 1685.

The harbour extends to the elevated bridge over the Loire built in 1903, the silhouette of which is a local landmark.

164 Between Niort and the coast of La Vendée on the Pertuis Breton there lies the extensive marshy region of the Marais Poitevien which is interlaced by canals, among them the Canal du Clain.

165 MORLAIX (Finistère) has been important to western Brittany since the Middle Ages both as a port and a market town. The railway viaduct, over 160 feet high, has been the dominant feature of this old-world town since 1861.

166 VANNES, the chief town of the Departement Morbihan and since 466 a bishop's see, was once the main centre of the Celtic Veneti (*Dariorigum Venetorum*). Bertone Nominoé, who was created Count of Vannes by Charlemagne, became Duke of Brittany in 826 and

brought about the political unification of the entire Armorican Peninsula. In the Middle Ages the Duchy, frequently supported by England, played an independent role. In 1532 the final unification of Brittany with France was proclaimed in Vannes.
On the eastern side of the town the town walls, built in the thirteenth century and renovated in the seventeenth, have been preserved together with the Tour du Connétable (fourteenth and fifteenth centuries). In place of the former moat there are now gardens *à la française*; in the background is the cathedral of Saint-Pierre.

167 Breton women at the PARDON OF SAINTE-BARBE in Le Faouet (Morbihan). Here in Brittany, as in no other part of France, regional traditions and costumes have been preserved. These are particularly in evidence at the religious festivals of the many places of pilgrimage, the Pardons. The women of the different districts are distinguished by the many variations in their caps.

168 The fishing harbour of LE CROISIC (Loire-Inférieure) has along its waterfront a row of houses built in the eighteenth century at the direction of the Duke of Aigullion, a minister of Louis XV.

169 The ALIGNEMENTS DU MÉNEC at CARNAC (Morbihan) extend for the greater part of a mile and comprise 1,099 *menhirs*, some of which are over 12 feet high. It is the largest collection of existing megalithic monuments of this kind, which are found both in Brittany and across the Channel in southern England.
In attempting to divine the purpose behind these stones, set up by a people who lived here before the Gauls, between 4,000 and 500 B.C., we are still compelled to fall back on guesswork.

170 On the road from Guingamp (Côtes-du-Nord) and Morlaix over the undulating country which falls away on the right towards the north coast of Brittany.

171 The village church of GUIMILIAU (Finistère) forms, together with its ancillary buildings, the "Enclos paroissial", a grouping characteristic of Breton religious architecture. Mediaeval tradition persisted here both in form and spirit until comparatively recent times. The calvary (Calvaire) of 1581–8 is the richest of its kind; the Passion is here represented in 200 figures.

172 The Calvary of PLOUGASTEL-DAOULAS (Finistère) in the extreme west of the Armorican Peninsula was erected in 1602–4 on the model of the Calvary of Guimiliau, to commemorate the ending of the plague of 1598. Our illustration shows the topmost part of the ensemble which has in all 180 figures. The village and its church were extensively damaged during the siege of the neighbouring harbour of Brest in August, 1944.

173 QUIMPER, the seat of the Prefecture of the Finistère Departement, used to be called Quimper-Corentin, in memory of its first bishop. St. Corentin was the companion of the legendary King Gradlon who is supposed to have come from Cornwall around the year 500 and made Quimper the principal town of the county of Cornouaille.
At the end of the Rue Keréon (i.e. Street of the Shoemakers), with its old overhanging houses, stands the cathedral of Saint-Corentin built in the thirteenth to fifteenth centuries, with spires dating from 1856.

174 VITRÉ (Ile-et-Vilaine), an old fortified town, stands on a hill by the banks of the Vilaine, and is dominated by its castle and the church tower of Notre-Dame. The castle, one of the best preserved mediaeval fortresses in Brittany, was built in the eleventh century and renovated in the fourteenth and fifteenth centuries. The barony of Vitré came to be linked from the thirteenth century onward with the county of Laval. The place, which was very difficult to capture, was a Huguenot stronghold. The Breton state representatives met here on several occasions between 1655 and 1706.

175 CAP FRÉHEL (Côtes-du-Nord) is a rocky promontory on the exceptionally indented north coast of Brittany.

176 FORT LA LATTE (Côtes-du-Nord), in the neighbourhood of Cap Fréhel, stands out upon a rocky headland in St. Malo Bay. The castle, built in the fourteenth century, and its massive centre tower, belonged to the lords of Matignon.

177 SAINT-MALO (Ile-et-Vilaine) is situated on a rocky peninsula at the mouth of the Rance, opposite Dinard. The town is named after a saint who came

from Britain in the sixth century and established a bishopric in the neighbouring Aleth (now St. Servan), a see which was transferred to St. Malo in 1140. This almost impregnable fastness held by bold seamen—it was besieged several times by the English without success—developed a particularly independent civic sense, with the motto "Ni Français, ni Bretons: Malouins!" In August, 1944 the picturesque old town girdled by walls dating from the twelfth century onwards, was almost entirely destroyed when the German garrison, acting on higher orders, defended itself although in a hopeless position, while the Americans were already advancing rapidly on Paris. In the middle of the expanse of ruins stands the damaged former cathedral of ST. VINCENT (parts of which date from the twelfth century). Its spire was formerly a characteristic feature of St. Malo.

178 The greater part of DINAN (Côtes-du-Nord), in the Middle Ages an important fortified place of the Duchy of Brittany, lies about 250 feet above the Rance. From the Jardin Anglais and the Lanvallay viaduct you can look down upon the old harbour quarter with its Gothic bridge.

179 MONT SAINT-MICHEL, a conical granite mass in the bay (Baie du Mont Saint-Michel) near the old town of Avranches, has served from ancient times as a shrine and a fortress. St. Aubert, Bishop of Avranches, built a chapel on the rock and dedicated it to the Archangel Michael. The holy mount owes its singular situation as an island castle connected with the land only at low tide, to an earthquake which occurred a year later. Following Aubert's miraculous deeds, pilgrimages began. In 966 the Duke of Normandy founded the Benedictine abbey. The sacred stronghold survived numerous sieges, and when fire destroyed the buildings, re-arose, more magnificent than before, thanks to the liberal gifts of the kings and the whole nation: the old house of prayer was replaced in the ninth century by the Carolingian church and in the eleventh by the Romanesque church, and the entire complex was finally crowned by the three-storeyed, Gothic monastery of the "Merveille", the cloisters and the lofty choir. Large numbers of boys from Germany made mass pilgrimages to Mont Saint-Michel from 1450 onwards. Since the reign of Louis XI the crypt has been used as a state prison. The slender spire on the central tower was added as recently as 1887, at the time of the restoration of the buildings.

180 BAYEUX (Calvados) was called *Augustodurun* up to the fourth century, and thereafter *Civitas Baiocassium*. In the ninth century the Normans became firmly established there. The CATHEDRAL OF NOTRE-DAME is one of the finest buildings in Normandy. The Romanesque church was largely destroyed by fire in 1105 and of it only the lower portions of the two west towers and the central nave have been preserved. The Gothic parts date from between the thirteenth and fifteenth centuries, when the nave was heightened, the choir, and the west front, the richly wrought south side and the centre tower built. Our photograph shows the south side looking towards the two west towers; on the right is the porch of the south transept (thirteenth century).

181 COUTANCES (Manche), the ancient *Cosedia*, was renamed *Constantia* at the end of the third century in honour of the Emperor Constantius Chlorus. In the fifth century it became a bishop's see. The Cathedral of Notre-Dame is one of the finest and purest creations of French Gothic architecture. Our picture shows the view down the nave (first quarter of the thirteenth century), and beneath the well-lit dome of the central tower towards the choir (mid-thirteenth century). About two-thirds of the small town of Coutances was destroyed in the fighting of 1944, including the immediate surroundings of the cathedral, but the cathedral itself remained practically intact.

182–3 CAEN, the chief town of the Departement Calvados with over 60,000 inhabitants, is (or was) rich in fine architecture and, thanks to its vigorous intellectual life, has gained the reputation of being a "Norman Athens". In the eleventh century Caen was the seat of the Norman Duke William, the conqueror of England, and was also preferred by his successors. Henry V of England used Caen as his Continental place of residence, and under his successor Henry VI preparations were made for founding a university there.

Between 1062 and 1066 William the Conqueror founded the church of ST. STEPHEN (Saint-Etienne or the Abbaye aux Hommes) as a penance for marrying a near relation, Queen Matilda, without a papal dispensation. At the same time the Queen founded at the other end of Caen the church of the Holy Trinity (Trinité or the Abbaye aux Dames).

The first Abbot of St. Etienne was the great school-man Lanfranc from Pavia, until in 1070 he became Archbishop of Canterbury. The church was consecrated in 1077, and in 1087 King William who had died in Rouen was buried here. The nave (Ill. 182) received its vaulting in the twelfth century and the Gothic choir was added early in the thirteenth. The church of SAINT-PIERRE (Ill. 183) stands in the midst of the extensive ruins left by the fighting of 1944 and was itself heavily damaged. This East aspect shows the most recent part of the church, on which rebuilding started in the thirteenth century: the apse, in highly decorative Renaissance style, was added by Hector Sohier during the years 1518 to 1545.

184 ROUEN, chief city of the Departement Seine-Inférieure with over 100,000 inhabitants, lies 80 miles from the mouth of the Seine and is both a sea and river port with important industries. In 841 the Northmen established themselves firmly in the former *Rotomagus* and in 911 made it the capital of Normandy. From 1066 to 1204 and 1419 to 1449 it was under English sovereignty and the English burnt Joan of Arc here in 1431.

Rouen suffered particularly severely in the second World War; a conflagration in June 1940 and the bombings of 1944 destroyed a great part of the town and its wealth of architectural monuments. Our post-war photograph shows the view from the left bank of the Seine looking towards the cathedral of Notre-Dame, a Gothic masterpiece; the spire of the centre tower is nineteenth-century. The restoration of the heavily damaged structure was put in hand immediately after the end of hostilities.

185 HONFLEUR (Calvados) has since the thirteenth century been a well-known fishing harbour at the mouth of the Seine, opposite Cherbourg. By the Bassin de l'Ouest or Vieux-Bassin, the centre of old Honfleur, there stands on a little island the LIEUTENANCE, all that remains of the sixteenth-century castle, where the King's representative had his residence. On the left of the picture in the background is the roof of the church of Sainte-Catherine, a fifteenth-century wooden structure.

186 A Norman farmhouse with a thatched roof. Normandy is first and foremost farming country with many fruit trees (cider), much livestock raising and dairy farming.

187 LE MANS, principal town of the county and later of the province of Maine, is now the seat of the Prefecture of the Sarthe Departement and has some 100,000 inhabitants. On the east side of the spacious Place des Jacobins on a slight eminence stands the CATHEDRAL OF SAINT JULIEN, built since the twelfth century; the fine Gothic choir dates from the first half of the thirteenth century. The church's foundation goes back to the time of the first bishop of Le Mans, Saint Julius, in the third and fourth centuries.

188 LAVAL, chief town of the Departement Mayenne, grew from the eleventh century onwards around the castle of the barons of Laval, who in 1429 became counts. The family of Montmorency became lords of the place in 1218; it later passed to the Montforts, the Colignys and the La Trémouilles.

From the Quai Paul Boudet a good view is obtained of the thirteenth-century Gothic Pont Vieux and the Vieux-Château, the old seat of the Counts of Laval, on the right bank of the Mayenne. The round fortress tower with its walls up to thirteen feet thick, and the more important other parts of the castle date from the eleventh and twelfth centuries.

189 The town of LOUVIERS (Eure), once the seat of the Dukes of Normandy, and given by Richard Cœur-de-Lion to the Archbishop of Rouen, built up its reputation for the manufacture of cloth and clothing in the thirteenth century. Over a third of the town was destroyed in the 1939–45 war, but fortunately the church of Notre-Dame situated in the centre was spared. The thirteenth-century Gothic structure possesses on its south side a porch richly decorated with figures; this masterpiece of the *flamboyant* style was built at the end of the fifteenth century.

190 The name of NOGENT-LE-ROTROU (Eure-et-Loir), the *Novigentum* of the Gallo-Roman period, recalls that of Rotrou, the first Count of Perche. The donjon,

built in the first half of the eleventh century, still dominates the town. In the foreground are the vege-table and fruit gardens of the fertile valley of the River Huisne.

191 CALAIS (Pas-de-Calais), the most important harbour for traffic with England, industrial town and fortress, lies 22 miles from Dover at the Channel's narrowest point. The former fishing village first acquired some importance in the twelfth century and joined the Hanseatic League in 1303. In 1346 the English besieged what had by then become a wealthy com-mercial town. When after a heroic defence lasting almost a year capitulation became inevitable because food supplies were giving out, six of the leading burghers presented themselves, with nooses about their necks and bearing the keys of the town, to the English king, Edward III, so as to prevent by their personal sacrifice the massacre of the rest of the in-habitants; the intervention of the good Queen Philippa, however, saved them from execution. Auguste Rodin created his fine memorial to the "Bourgeois de Calais" in 1895; it stands in front of the former Town Hall on the Place d'Armes, in the centre of the old town by the harbour which was almost completely razed during the second World War. (Other castings of the bronze memorial are to be found beside the Houses of Parliament in London and in Basle.)

192 At ETRETAT (Siene-Inférieure) the Pays de Caux drops steeply down to the Channel (La Manche), the waves of which beat against the cliffs. The view is of the bathing beach looking towards the Falaise d'Amont.

193 ABBEVILLE (Somme) developed from a settlement of the Abbey of Saint-Riquier (hence the name *Abbatis villa*), acquired its town wall under Hugh Capet and became the seat of the Counts of Ponthieu. The town, which was damaged by bombing already in 1918, was largely destroyed in the second World War. In the midst of the ruins stands the damaged abbey church of Saint-Vulfran, which was begun in the late Gothic style in 1488 and was given an elaborate west front.

194–5 ARRAS, chief town of the Departement Pas-de-Calais and of the former County of Artois, the land of the Atrebates, belonged in the Middle Ages by turns to Flanders, France (from 1180), Burgundy, the Habs-burgs and finally, since 1659, to France. Several peace treaties were signed here. During the war of 1914–18 Arras stood for years in the firing line and was heavily damaged; the town was nevertheless suc-cessfully restored true to style. The Place des Héros (formerly the Petite Place) and the Grande Place in particular have preserved their Flemish character. The uniform gabled fronts of the houses, parts of which date from the Middle Ages, are seventeenth century. Ill. 194 shows the Place des Héros as seen from the Town Hall, with the tower of the Church of St. John the Baptist in the background. Ill. 195 is a view between the pillars of the arcades which run round all four sides of the two squares.

196–7 BEAUVAIS, the chief town of the Departement Oise, derived its name from the tribe of the Belloraci. In the ninth century it became the seat of a county, which in 1013 passed to the Bishops of Beauvais. The Gothic Cathedral of SAINT PIERRE was begun in 1227 on such a gigantic scale that only the choir (nearly 160 feet high) was completed; the transept was added in the first half of the sixteenth century, but the main nave is lacking. The structure surpasses all earlier efforts in its grandeur of conception but it also went beyond the bounds of the technical possibilities of the time with the result that the construction of supports soon became necessary. It is nevertheless, even in its fragmentary state, one of the boldest of Gothic crea-tions. During the war of 1939–45 the centre of Beau-vais was almost entirely destroyed but the cathedral escaped with minor damage. Ill. 196 shows the post-war view from the north-east, which has been opened up by the destruction of buildings. Ill. 197 is a view of the south porch, with to the left the fortified gate-way of the former bishop's palace (now courts of justice) dating from the fourteenth century.

198 AMIENS, seat of the Prefecture of the Somme Departe-ment with over 80,000 inhabitants, the old capital of Picardy, was named after the Belgic tribe of the Ambiani and was originally called *Samarobriva*, i.e. bridge over the Somme. Saint Firmin the Con-fessor lived and worked here in the third to fourth centuries as the first bishop. In the Middle Ages the town was partly under the authority of a count and

partly under a bishop. In 1185 it came under the French Crown and temporarily also under Burgundy and the Spanish Habsburgs. In the 1914–18 war it was occupied by the Germans, retaken by the French after the Battle of the Marne, and heavily bombarded in the German spring offensive of 1918. During the second World War considerably greater damage was inflicted and almost the entire centre of the town was destroyed; but on this occasion too the CATHEDRAL OF NOTRE-DAME, one of the greatest monuments of mediaeval Christendom, was spared. In competition with the great Gothic cathedrals of northern France which had been begun earlier, there arose here from 1220 onwards this edifice of High Gothic, designed by Robert de Luzarches, of vaster proportions and more unified in conception and execution than any other of its kind. In 1236 the nave and façade were already completed, by 1247 the choir and its surrounding chapels. The three west porches—the centre one of which has the figure of Christ teaching ("le Beau Dieu d'Amiens"), here illustrated—represent with their wealth of statuary one of the greatest achievements of thirteenth-century sculpture.

199 SOISSONS (Aisne), the ancient *Noviodunum*, was the capital of the Seussiones. Clovis defeated the Romans here in 486, and in 511 Soissons became the residence of the Merovingian king of Neustria, whose kingdom was later taken over by the Frank Pepin the Short in 752. This strategically important place was much fought over in the war of 1914–18, in the course of which the façade of SAINT-JEAN-DES-VIGNES was damaged. Our picture shows all that was left of the great abbey church after the demolitions of the nineteenth century. The lower part is late thirteenth century, the part above it with the rose window opening, fourteenth century; the north tower was completed as late as 1520.

200 LAON, the chief town of the Departement Aisne, stands on an isolated hill in the broad plain of Champagne. St. Remigius installed the first bishop here in 497 and his successors played the part of temporal lords of the place up to 1790. The last of the Carolingians built their residence here in the tenth century. Constituting the landmark of the town with its elegant openwork towers, stands the former cathedral of Notre-Dame, which dates from the twelfth and thirteenth centuries; it can be seen from far away on the old battlefields of northern France.

201 SENLIS (Oise), once a settlement of the Silvanectes, a quiet little provincial town just over 25 miles north of Paris, was from the fourth century (St. Regulus) until 1801 a bishop's see. The Carolingians had a royal residence here, and in 987 Hugh Capet had himself elected King of France at Senlis. The town was damaged in both World Wars. Beyond the Church of St. Pierre can be seen the choir and tower of the Cathedral of Notre-Dame (twelfth and thirteenth centuries).

202 NOYON (Oise) has since the sixth century been the see of a bishop who was also the temporal lord of the town. Nowadays it is, together with Senlis, suffragan to the bishopric of Beauvais. In Noyon Charlemagne had himself crowned King of Neustria in 768.
On the north side of the imposing Early Gothic Cathedral of Notre-Dame stands the "Librairie" or library of the cathedral chapter, a wooden structure dating from about the year 1500.

203–4 RHEIMS (Marne), the ancient *Durocortorum*, tribal centre of the Remi and capital of the Roman province of Belgica secunda, the old cultural centre of Champagne with its wealth of wines, was for centuries the town where the French kings were crowned. Around the year 300 St. Sixtus founded a bishopric here, and his successor, St. Remigius, here baptized in 496 Clovis the Merovingian, founder of the Frankish Empire; on the latter occasion a dove is reputed to have descended from heaven bearing an ampulla containing the holy unguent with which the rulers of France were anointed in the cathedral after their coronation. On 17th July, 1429, Charles VII was crowned in the presence of Joan of Arc, after she had taken the town from the English.
The CATHEDRAL OF NOTRE-DAME, the south tower of which (Ill. 204) rises above the rather aristocratic neighbouring streets, is, as befits the national shrine of the French, the splendid climax of cathedral architecture as a whole. Its decorative sculpture, combining Gothic spirituality with classical dignity, survived even the storms of the French Revolution, to which the carved figures of most of the other cathedrals of France (with the exception of Chartres and Amiens)

fell victim. Not even the heavy shelling of the 1914–18 war managed to detract permanently from the general impressiveness of this great edifice.

The equestrian statue of Joan of Arc by Paul Dubois (1896), which originally graced the centre of the Square in front of the cathedral, was re-erected on one side of the Square, in front of the Courts of Justice, on the occasion of the celebrations which marked the completion of the restoration of the cathedral in 1938.

205 A lock on a canal in Champagne (cf. Ills. 108 and 207). Among the waterways forming the great French network are the East canal (262 miles), the Rhine-Rhône Canal (205 miles), the Rhine-Marne Canal (196 miles), the Burgundy Canal (151 miles), the South Canal (150 miles) and the Central Canal (72 miles).

206 MEAUX (Seine-et-Marne), tribal centre of the Meldi and later the principal town of the Brie region, is now a modest provincial town within the orbit of Paris, 25 miles away. The Cathedral of Saint-Etienne (twelfth and sixteenth centuries) is mirrored in the quiet waters of the Marne which here takes a bend. The most famous bishop to occupy this see, created in the fourth century, was the famous preacher Bossuet (1681–1704).

207 LANGRES (Haute-Marne) lies on a northern spur of the Plateau de Langres in a strategically favourable position, the value of which was early recognised by the Romans. From the twelfth to the eighteenth century the bishops, as temporal lords of the county of Langres, were members of the French peerage. The Marne and the Saône both have their source near Langres, and the two rivers are connected by a canal 140 miles long, which was cut between 1880 and 1890. From the heights on which the town stands you can look eastward across to the Lecey reservoir which was built to provide water for the canal in the valley of the Liez, a small tributary of the Marne.

208 NANCY, the principal city of the Departement of Meurthe-et-Moselle with over 100,000 inhabitants, the seat of a bishop and a university, developed as late as the twelfth to fourteenth centuries from an insignificant hamlet into a town, and after 1477 was transformed by the Dukes of Lorraine into the brilliant capital city of their territory. Duke Leopold who succeeded to the dukedom in 1697, contributed greatly to the improvement of his residence until in 1736 he became Emperor through his marriage with Maria Theresa and moved to Vienna. Nancy then became until 1766 the seat of the Polish king Stanislaus Lesczynski who was under French protection; after his death Lorraine became a solely French possession. Under Stanislaus the Place Stanislas (1752–60)—the former Place Royale—was laid out. With its palace buildings, fountains and partly gilded wrought-iron railings, it became one of the most delightful Squares deriving from the eighteenth century. (Emmanuel Héré, a pupil of Boffrand, was the architect; the wrought-iron-work was designed by Jean Lamour.) In the middle of the Square is a statue of King Stanislaus by Jacquot; in 1831 it was put up in place of the statue which Stanislaus had erected to his son-in-law, Louis XV of France.

209 To the west of the Route des Crêtes near Hohneck the ridges and valleys of the High Vosges (Vosges cristallines) stretch as far as the eye can see.

210 The road between Altkirch and Belfort offers a wide view southwards towards the Swiss frontier region and the foothills of the Jura.

211 GUEBWILLER, in German Gebweiler (Haut-Rhin), is one of the small Alsatian towns lying amid the vineyards of the eastern foothills of the Vosges. In the Middle Ages this fortified town was subject to the Princely Abbots of Murbach. The church of Saint-Leger (St. Leodgar), like most Alsatian buildings constructed of the red sandstone of the Vosges, presents with its west front a fine example of the work of the twelfth century Rhenish-Romanesque school.

212 RIQUEWIHR, in German Reichenweier (Haut-Rhin), famed for its Riesling wines, has preserved in its Grande Rue the perfect picture of a small Upper Alsatian town; several neighbouring towns and villages were destroyed in the fighting during 1944–5. The Dukes of Württemberg remained in possession of the domain of Riquewihr from the fourteenth to the

eighteenth century; one of them mortgaged his vineyards to enable him to make a loan to Voltaire.

213 SÉLESTAT, German Schlettstadt (Bas-Rhin), was a Carolingian royal residence, and Charlemagne celebrated Christmas here in 775. It became an Imperial city under the Emperor Frederick II. In the fifteenth and sixteenth centuries a famous school of humanists was established here, which counted Erasmus of Rotterdam among its students. Under the Peace of Westphalia the town was awarded to the French who had kept it occupied since 1634; Louis XIV had it fortified by Vauban. The church of St. George distinguishes itself from the town's other mediaeval church by its fine Gothic tower.

214 COLMAR, chief town of the Departement Haut-Rhin with over 40,000 inhabitants, became an Imperial city in 1226, enjoyed the protection of Rudolf of Habsburg and resisted the efforts of the Bishop of Strasbourg to achieve hegemony. In 1354 it formed, together with nine other imperial cities, the League of the Ten Towns. The old part of the town, with its buildings of the fourteenth to the seventeenth centuries, forms the perfect setting for those unique masterpieces of painting produced on Alsatian soil and here preserved the pictures of Martin Schongauer and the Isenheim Altar by Mathias Grünewald. The Market Hall, Alsatian Koifhus, French Ancienne Douane, dates from 1480.

215 ZELLENBERG (Haut-Rhin), formerly a fortified village, stands on a hill in the Alsatian wine and fruit-growing district among the eastern foothills of the Vosges.

216 STRASBOURG, German Strassburg, chief city of the Departement Bas-Rhin with a population of some 175,000, was the *Argentoratum* of the Romans; in 496 it became Frankish, in 843 Lotharingian and in 1262 a free Imperial city. In the fifteenth century it achieved its zenith as the centre of humanism and German mysticism. The burghers established their rights in the face of the opposing power of the Bishop. After the Emperor had, through the Peace of Westphalia, abandoned his claim to sovereignty, Louis XIV marched into Strasbourg in 1681. In 1770 and 1771 Goethe studied law at the famous university founded in 1538. In his essay *Von deutscher Baukunst* he describes the great experience of Gothic art and architecture which the minster had afforded him. In August 1870 Strasbourg was invested by the Germans and from 1871 to 1918 it was the capital of the Imperial Province of Alsace-Lorraine. From 1940 to 1944 it was once again occupied by German troops. As the meeting-place of the Council of Europe Strasbourg, while fully loyal to France and maintaining faithfully its Alsatian character, has undertaken a new mission to promote closer ties between the nations—one to which it seems peculiarly predestined.

The old-world Rue Mercière is dominated at one end by the magnificent west front of the MINSTER (Cathédrale Notre-Dame). The building of the façade was begun in 1277; in 1284 Erwin von Steinbach—later eulogized by Goethe—undertook the direction of the work, and by 1291 it had progressed as far as the great rose-windows; the building of the two towers took until 1365. The rich sculpture on the west porches, which has been preserved, dates back to the thirteenth and fourteenth centuries.

INDEX

Abbeville . . 193
Agde . . . 96
Aigues-Mortes .93, 94
Aix-en-Provence . 86
Ajaccio . . 72
Albi . . . 112
Aliscamps, Les . 84
Amboise . . 149
Amiens . . 198
Angers. . . 162
Angoulême . . 132
Annecy . . 51
Antibes . . 64
Arles . . 82, 84
Arras . . 194, 195
Arve (River). . 53
Autun . . 34
Auxerre . . 29
Avallon . . 32
Avignon . 89–91

Banyuls . 100, 101
Bastia . . 71, 77
Baux, Les . 78, 79
Bavella, Col de . 74
Bayeux . . 180
Bayonne . . 107
Beauce (Countryside) 25
Beaune . . 38
Beauvais . 196, 197
Béziers . . . 98
Blois . . . 148
Bonifacio . . 75
Bordeaux . . 118
Bourg-en-Bresse . 43
Bourges . . 142
Briançon . . 56
Brou (Bourg-en-Bresse) . . 43
Burgundy (Farmstead) 36

Caen . . 182, 183
Cahors. . . 114
Calais . . . 191
Carcassonne . 109, 110
Carnac . . 169
Cassis . . 70
Castellane . . 60
Cérons . . 108

Chablis . 30, 31
Chaise-Dieu, La . 133
Chambord . . 150
Chamonix, Valley of 53, 54
Chantilly . 13, 14
Charente (River) . 131
Chartres . 23, 24
Chartreuse, La Grande, 52
Chartreuse du Liget 161
Chaumont . . 151
Chenonceau . . 153
Cher (River). . 153
Cheverny . . 152
Chinon . . 156
Cirque de Gavarnie 104
Cognac . . 131
Collioure . . 102
Colmar . . 214
Compiègne . . 22
Conques . . 122
Corniche, La Grande (Riviera) . . 63
Côte-d'Or . . 37
Corsica . 71–77
Coutances . . 181
Croisic, Le . . 168

Dijon . . . 39
Dinan . . . 178
Dôle . . . 40
Doubs (River) 41, 42
Durance (River) . 59

Elne . . . 97
Embrun . . 57
Erbalunga . . 76
Etretat . . 192
Evian-les-Bains . 50
Eyzies-de-Tayac, Les 127

Foix . . . 103
Fontainebleau 20, 21
Fontevrault . . 157
Fort La Latte . 176
Fréhel, Cap . . 175

Gard (River) . 85
Garonne (River) . 118

Gartempe (River) . 159
Gavarnie, Cirque de 104
Geneva, Lake of . 50
Gien . . . 147
Grasse . . . 62
Grenoble . . 49
Guebwiller . . 211
Guéry, Lac de . 137
Guimiliau . . 171

Hérault (River) . 96
Honfleur . . 185

Indre (River) . 160
Isère (River) . . 49
Isle (River) . . 130

Langres . . 207
Laon . . . 200
Laval . . . 188
Loire (River), 146, 147, 149, 163
Louviers . . 189
Lyons . . 45

Macon . . 46
Mans, Le . . 187
Marais Poitevien . 164
Marne (River) . 206
Marseilles . . 68
Martigues . . 92
Martin, Cap. . 65
Mayenne (River) . 188
Meaux . . 206
Menton . . 67
Mer de Glace . 55
Millau . . 125, 126
Moissac . . 116
Montauban . . 113
Mont Blanc . . 54
Mont-Dore, Le . 138
Montmajour . . 87
Montréjeau . . 106
Mont-St-Michel . 179
Monts Dômes . 140
Morlaix . . 165
Moulins . . 141
Murat . . . 134

Musculdy . . 105

Nancy . . . 208
Nantes. . . 163
Nevers . . . 145
Nice . . . 66
Nîmes . . . 83
Nogent-le-Rotrou . 190
Noyon . . 202

Orb (River) . . 98
Orange . . 80
Orléans . . 146

Paris . . 2–10, 12
Périgueux . . 130
Perpignan . . 99
Piana, Calanche de 73
Plougastel-Daoulas. 172
Poitiers . . 155
Pont du Gard . 85
Pont-St-Esprit . 47
Puy, Le . 135, 136

Quimper . . 173

Raincy, Le . . 11
Rambouillet . 19
Rance (River) . 178
Rheims . 203, 204
Rhône (River) 47, 88, 89
Riquewihr . . 212
Rochelle, La 128, 129
Rocher Sanadoire . 139
Rouen . . . 184

Saint-Benoît-sur-Loire . . 143
Sainte-Barbe . . 167
Sainte-Enimie . 123
Saint-Emilion . 119
Saint-Gilles . . 95
Saint-Malo . . 177
Saint-Rémy-de-Provence . . 81
Saint-Savin-sur-Gartempe . 158, 159
Saint-Seine-l'Abbaye 35
Salins-les-Bains . 44
Sanary-sur-Mer . 69

Saône (River) . 46
Sélestat . . 213
Seine (River) 7, 8, 184
Senlis . . . 201
Sisteron . . 59
Soissons . . 199
Souillac . . 117
Strasbourg . . 216

Sully-sur-Loire . 144

Tarascon . . 88
Tarn (River) 112, 113, 123–125

Toulouse . . 115
Tours . . . 154
Troyes . . . 28

Vannes . . 166
Verdon (River) . 61
Versailles . 15–18
Vézelay . . 33
Vézère (River) . 127
Vienne. . . 48
Villefranche-de-Rouergue . . 121

Villeneuve-sur-Yonne . . 27
Vitré . . . 174
Vosges. . . 209

Yonne (River) . 26, 29

Zellenberg . . 215

INDEX OF PICTURES ACCORDING TO DEPARTEMENTS

Ain 43
Aisne 199, 200
Allier 141
Alpes-Maritimes 62–67
Ariège 103
Aube 28
Aude 109, 110
Aveyron 121, 122, 125, 126
Bas-Rhin 213, 216
Basses-Pyrénées 105, 107
Bouches-du-Rhône . 68, 70, 78, 79, 81, 82, 84, 86–88, 92
Calvados 180, 182, 185
Cantal 134
Charente 131, 132
Charente-Maritime 128, 129
Cher 142
Cher-et-Loire 154
Corse 71–77
Côte-d'Or 35–39
Côtes-du-Nord 170, 175, 176, 178
Dordogne 127, 130
Doubs 41, 42
Eure 189
Eure-et-Loir 23–25, 190
Finistère 165, 171–173
Gard 47, 83, 85, 93–95
Gironde 108, 118–120
Hautes Alpes 56–58
Haute Garonne 106, 115
Haute Loire 133, 135, 136
Haute Marne 207
Hautes Pyrénées 104
Haut Rhin 211, 212, 214, 215
Haute Savoie 50–51, 53–55
Hérault 96, 98
Ille-et-Vilaine 174, 177
Indre-et-Loire . . 149, 153, 154, 156, 160, 161
Isère 48, 49, 52
Jura 40, 44
Loir-et-Cher 148, 150–152
Loire-Inférieure 163, 168
Loiret 143, 144, 146, 147
Lot 114, 117
Lozère 123, 124
Maine-et-Loire 157, 162
Manche 179, 181
Marne 203, 204
Mayenne 188
Meurthe-et-Moselle 208
Morbihan 166, 167, 169
Nièvre 145
Oise 13–14, 22, 196, 197, 201, 202
Pas-de-Calais 191, 194, 195
Puy-de-Dôme 137–140
Pyrénées-Orientales 97, 99–102
Rhône 45
Saône-et-Loire 34, 46
Sarthe 187
Seine 2–10, 12
Seine-Inférieure 184, 192
Seine-et-Marne 20–21, 206
Seine-et-Oise 11, 15–19
Somme 193, 198
Tarn 111, 112
Var 69
Vaucluse 80, 89–91
Vendée 164
Vienne 155, 158, 159
Vosges 209
Yonne 26–27, 29–33